Ceremonies

for life

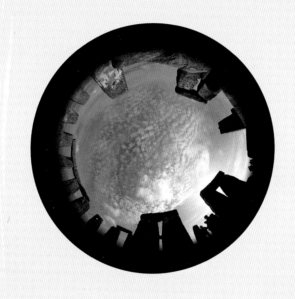

Ceremonies
for life

MICHAEL JORDAN

COLLINS & BROWN

First published in Great Britain in 2001
by Collins & Brown Limited
London House
Great Eastern Wharf
Parkgate Road
London SW11 4NQ

Distributed in the United States and Canada by Sterling Publishing Co,
387 Park Avenue South, New York, NY10016, USA

1 3 5 7 9 8 6 4 2

British Library Cataloguing-in-Publication Data:
A catalogue record for this book is available from the British Library.

ISBN 1 85585 794 4

Commissioned by Liz Dean
Project managed by Claire Wedderburn-Maxwell
Designed by Sue Miller
Edited by Annie Lee
Commissioned photography on pages 2, 42–5, 93–99, 118–9 by Nicki Dowey
Picture research by Collins & Brown and Zooid Pictures Limited

Colour reproduction by Global Colour Ltd, Malaysia
Printed by C&C Offset Ltd, Hong Kong

Contents

Introduction to alternative ceremonies 6
The origins of alternative ceremonies 8

CHAPTER ONE 12
What you need to perform alternative ceremonies
Preparing to perform ceremonies 14
Sacred spaces and sacred circles 16
What tools do I need? 18
Sharing or working alone? 20
Why we should perform rituals 22
The spiritual significance of trees 24
Honouring sacred sites 26

CHAPTER TWO 28
Rites of passage
Celebrating the transitions of life 30
A ceremony to mark conception 32
Ceremonies to celebrate birth 34
Welcoming the new arrival 36
Saining or naming your baby 38
Planting a tree for the birth of a baby 40
Birthstones for a new-born baby 42
Birth ceremonies in tribal societies 46
Miscarriage and stillbirth 48
Later rites of passage – puberty 50
Celebrating the menopause 52

CHAPTER THREE 54
Ceremonies to mark death and rebirth
Journey to the otherworld 56
Egyptian rituals of the dead 58
Native American rites for the dead 60
Polynesian and Eastern funeral traditions 62
Chinese and Japanese funeral rites 64
Tailoring to the individual 66
Woodland and personalized burials 68
Ancient sacred sites 70

CHAPTER FOUR 72
Ceremonies to honour the cycle of nature
Ceremonies of the natural world 74
Invocation to the Goddess in Wicca 76

The Wheel of the Year 78
Celebrating the spring 80
Ceremonies to celebrate midsummer 82
Welcoming the harvest 84
Rites to perform at the equinoxes 86
A ceremony for the midwinter solstice 88
The Yule log: light in the darkness 90

CHAPTER FIVE 92
Celebrating marriage and other relationships
Alternative ways to celebrate marriage 94
A simple wedding ceremony 98
The sacred marriage in Wicca 100
A folk marriage from India 102
A European wedding ceremony 104
A ritual of separation 106

CHAPTER SIX 108
Performing alternative ceremonies
The significance of propitiation and prayer 110
Rituals of purification 112
Using herbs for rituals 114
Herbs and plants for different occasions 116
Sacrifice: a rite of reverence 118
The value of prayer 120
Rituals for healing 122
Alleviating stress through meditation 124
Basic yoga positions 126
Chakras and breathing 128
The power of dance 130
The power of chanting 132
Eastern ritual techniques 134

Conclusion 136
The Law 138
Liferites 139
Useful information 140
Acknowledgements 141
Index 142

Introduction to
alternative ceremonies

Shortly before she died in 1999, one of the truly respected and international pioneers of modern paganism, Doreen Valiente, talked to me of her personal faith.

Doreen was a member of Wicca, the spiritual revival of what she called the Old Religion, a renewal begun in the 1950s of trust in the God and Goddess of the natural world. At a time when, on a previous occasion in her life, severe illness had brought her close to death, she was comforted not by Christianity or any other conventional religion that we would call *orthodox*, but by her belief in witchdom, the Land of the Faery.

When Doreen thought that her candle flame was about to flicker out, she had felt herself transported to a starlit winter woodland and a stockade from which arose a beautiful blue radiance. It was, as she put it, nothing to do with any Christian heaven, or any spiritualist Summerland, or anything else. She was off to her own kind.

Doreen Valiente wanted her faith in Wicca honoured to the last, and when she died she was laid to rest in accordance with her wishes, without so much as a word from a conventional priest or minister. Her passing was marked with sadness and joy, and she was remembered in the way that she had celebrated most of the defining moments of her life, through alternative ceremony.

The meaning of 'pagan'

We should understand, briefly, what 'pagan' means because the word tends to imply different things to different people. Look in a dictionary and a pagan is one who has no religion or is a heathen. For many Christians the word equates, quite erroneously, with Devil worship, but it actually comes from an archaic Italian term, *pagani*, meaning 'the people of the land', and was used by the first orthodox Christians in a derogatory sense against anyone who was too 'rustic' to convert to Christianity! Today, as entrenched religious dogma becomes *passé*, words like pagan and orthodox seem increasingly meaningless and will, I believe, be relegated ultimately to history.

Pagan alternatives include Wicca, the main branch of pagan revival to which most modern witches adhere, and Druidry, the collective name for a diverse group of organizations, not all of which are pagan, following the religious traditions of the pre-Christian Celts. A number of others exist today, including Asatru, the revival of the old Scandinavian and Germanic religions, and Shamanism, the most ancient form of spirituality based on principles of animism, which recognizes that all objects in nature possess souls and are controlled by spirit guardians.

Why we need alternative ceremonies

An alternative funeral was Doreen Valiente's preference, but why should *any* of us seek alternative ceremonies and how can they help us? A growing band of ordinary people the world over, from all walks of life, are finding the rituals laid down by Church and State increasingly irrelevant. They see the conventional monotheistic faiths straitjacketed by outmoded dogma and ritual, out of touch with today's spiritual needs and

Through taking part in alternative ceremonies we are able to reach out and open channels to the spiritual world.

insufficiently focused on the real challenges facing the modern world. Not least of their worries is the harm being inflicted on the natural world in which we live, a pressing issue barely addressed by Judaism, Christianity or Islam. The eastern faiths of Hinduism and Buddhism fall short in other respects. There is an increasing and justifiable concern about the irrevocable damage being caused by deforestation, the waste of precious non-sustainable natural resources, the excessive use of hydrocarbon fuels leading to the Greenhouse Effect and, latterly, the potential risk in developing genetically modified crops.

Alternative ceremonies can offer us wonderful and also *individual* ways of celebrating and remembering the important times in our experience: growing to maturity, making partnerships, having children, coping with old age and, ultimately, marking our deaths. They allow us to open channels to the spiritual world and to express our joy and thanks for being alive, but also to rid ourselves of negative influences that can bring on stress, fatigue and illness.

Through the ceremonies described and explained here we can articulate our personal beliefs, irrespective of whether we conform to orthodoxy, a nature-based spirituality or possess no formal belief at all. Even if we consider that our lives are devoid of spirituality, such ceremonies can still be of value because it would appear that, underneath, we all possess a desire for some kind of ritual to help us reach a meaning about the purpose of our lives.

The origins of
alternative ceremonies

The ceremonies included in this book encompass many celebrations and rituals, reflecting a level of individual freedom and choice about how we honour and revere the powers of the spirit world. However, this spiritual freedom has often been won at a price.

Article 18 of the Universal Declaration of Human Rights states that 'Everyone has the right to freedom of thought, conscience and religion; this right includes freedom to change his religion or belief, and freedom, either alone or in community with others and in public or private, to manifest his religion or belief in teaching practice, worship and observance.' It has not always been so.

During the Middle Ages the Church of Rome, largely supported by the Protestant movement, argued that such freedom was tantamount to a blasphemous pact with the Devil, and frequently it earned the attentions of the Inquisition. Many of the things for which we have won acceptance were once classed as capital offences and, at the very least, earned torture at the hands of the Church authorities.

It was not until 1951, in England, that successive legal statutes against witchcraft were replaced by the Fraudulent Mediums Act, giving freedom for individuals to practise alternative rites so long as they did not result in harm to persons or property. Similar liberalization took place elsewhere in Europe and the rest of the Christian world. In reality, though, public sentiment was still very much against any notion of alternative religion, and to be, for example, a self-confessed witch was a courageous act even in the 1970s. Today, many members of the Christian Church remain implacably opposed to religious ceremonies of an unorthodox nature.

The pioneers of religious freedom

Much of the breakthrough was born out of the courage and vision of just a few individuals like Gerald Gardner, Alex Sanders and Doreen Valiente, who openly professed belief in paganism. They were pioneers who believed that we have lost our spiritual paths but can perhaps find them again away from the entrenched and formalized 'orthodox religious' ceremonies of living and dying. They chose to follow alternatives that do not conform to any of the major orthodox religions, including Judaism, Christianity and Islam. Many of those to whom we owe a debt of gratitude for today's freedoms had to follow their beliefs in secret for much of their lives to avoid persecution. They believed, passionately, however, that each and every person has that right to worship and practise their chosen faith in whatever way they think fit, without fear of censorship or repression.

We may find inspiration in the following places:

- beside the ocean
- beneath the spreading branches of a great tree
- on the shore of a lake

Gardner, born in Lancashire in 1884, was the founder of the modern Wicca movement and we owe much of the present-day 'manual' of alternative ceremonies to his efforts and inspiration. He possessed a strong interest in overseeing the revival of the ancient and time-honoured craft of the witch and in making it available to the person-in-the-street. He incorporated a considerable amount of ritual into a book, *Witchcraft Today*, first published in 1954. Similar innovations were brought by such organizations as the Ancient Druid Order, founded in 1717, whose teaching rests on a love of nature and the view that spirituality should be an integral part of daily life. It was this body that campaigned successfully in the early years of the twentieth century to be allowed to worship freely at the ancient monument of Stonehenge in the south of England.

Some people may associate alternative ceremonies which are carried out on a fairly intimate and local basis with the activities of cults, some of which have earned questionable reputations in recent years. We can practise our own rites of passage and offer tokens of appeasement or gratitude to whatever spiritual forces control our lives without belonging to any religious organization. Our celebrations do not oblige us to live in opt-out communes, wear distinctive dress, hand over money or possess convictions that many would regard as eccentric and even dangerous.

Where have our ceremonies come from?

We can be inventive in our alternative ceremonies. They need not have come from anywhere other than our own creative imaginations! This means that we can tailor small rituals very much to our own lifestyles and purposes. All that is demanded of us is that we remain within the law and keep to reasonable confines of propriety. So lighting a bonfire and dancing around it naked to welcome the spring is acceptable if you have a large and secluded back garden in which to conduct your invocation. It is probably less of a good idea if you are reliant on using the local football pitch as temporary hallowed ground. At the end of the book is a section dealing with your rights under the law that should clarify the more important rules about what you can and cannot do within present legislation.

Ceremonies can be invented on the spur of the moment, without any deference to past tradition or, by and large, present religious rules and regulations. Nonetheless many of the rites have their roots in the distant past. In the Christian world a considerable number, based on old customs and folklore, can be traced to our pagan ancestors. In Europe this often means looking back at the religious beliefs and mythology of the Celts, the Vikings and the Germanic races. In Africa tribal culture is a much more recent reality and its rituals are widely practised. Elsewhere in the world, in the Americas and Australasia, we can still find a varying treasury of aboriginal or indigenous tradition on which to draw.

This does not mean that the alternative ceremonies we carry out today are, necessarily, authentic copies of ancient rites. More often than not, the details of what was done in pre-Christian times have been destroyed in the flames of bigotry and intolerance. What has replaced them is largely what we, through our romantic twentieth-century eyes, *imagine* such ancient rites to have been. There is nothing wrong with romance, but we should not delude ourselves that when, in Guildford, or Antwerp or Tallahassee, we perform a ceremony to celebrate the Summer Solstice we are faithfully reproducing something which Druids or Angles or Navajo Indians did in prehistory. The short answer is that,

The people who practice rites

■ Who are the practitioners of our alternative ceremonies? To a large extent they can include you and me! But there are others who claim particular qualifications — the priests and priestesses who have joined time-honoured fraternities and sororities. These are the people who act as celebrants, seers, healers and, in the case of shamanism, transporters of souls.

generally speaking, we don't know what they did. Ancient people did not publicize their most sacred rites and, in any case, the Christian writers who were supposed to act as the guardians of history often chose to debase the record through misinformation and ridicule.

Much of the practical ceremony that will be found in the following pages is therefore based on comparatively modern traditions established in Druidry and Wicca. This is not a reflection of any desire on my part to be selective, but merely because the two movements have generated more literature and therefore more detail than many others. Many of the practices are based on the knowledge and experience of men and women who have devoted their lifetimes to alternative ways of expressing spirituality. Other ceremonies have been gleaned from vestiges of local tradition around the world and from the advice of individuals who work on a purely personal understanding that owes nothing to any wider convention.

The practitioners, the 'priests' of alternative ceremony, are drawn from all walks of life, ranging from bank managers to shop-keepers, solicitors to bricklayers. Whatever their profession may be, these ceremonies find a personal appeal and validity. But there is another important aspect that we should not forget. Many of the traditions are vanishing as fast as the cultures that honoured them, for example Native American tribes and Siberian clans. They become adulterated or die out, and unless we protect and conserve the fragility of such ancient beliefs and rites we shall lose them for ever.

The place of alternative ceremonies

A few years ago the town of Milton Keynes in Buckinghamshire, England, made legal history when it consented to the purchase of land specifically for the purpose of holding the festivals of Wicca known as *Sabbats*. It was a major breakthrough in the liberalization of our right to religious freedom, won despite strenuous opposition from the Church.

In places as widely separated as remote mountain tops, fields and woodlands, gardens and inner city flats we now feel comfortable to celebrate events including the passing of the seasons, the Summer and Winter Solstices, the birth of a baby, growing up, marriage, parting and death. We give reverence to the natural world of trees and flowers, springs, lakes, and the sea. We perform solemn rituals to obstruct the passage of a new motorway through a piece of precious countryside, the destruction of an ancient forest, the uprooting of a hedgerow. Men and women, again free to work, weave their magic for the alleviation of suffering, for prosperity, for the safe return of a loved one. Nowhere escapes this tide of alternative ceremony.

Sometimes we feel it necessary to carry out such acts alone and in the privacy of our own thoughts, sometimes we come together as small initiated groups or covens, at others whole communities are openly encouraged to join in. Similar trends towards the practice of non-orthodox rites may be seen in other parts of the world.

The chapters which follow provide a step-by-step guide to the celebration of our most important 'staging posts' – the major events of life including birth, adolescence, marriage and death as well as the changing rhythms of nature.

■ **There are other means of raising or alerting the forces of the spirit world that do not necessarily involve the services of priest or shaman but include prayer and, most importantly, dance, used since prehistoric times. In Wicca, it is one of the Eightfold Paths designed to raise the supernatural powers and to release latent spiritual forces which lie dormant within the human body.**

CHAPTER I

What you need
to perform
alternative ceremonies

It is one of the real delights of

alternative ceremonies that we

are wholly free to make our own

choices within the legal limitations

of the country in which we live.

We are not subject to the

petty restrictions placed upon

ceremonies conducted under

the banners of orthodoxy.

Preparing to
perform ceremonies

One of the objections raised by many people to undergoing rites of baptism, marriage or burial under the aegis of the Christian Church is that the words of its ceremonies, if we take them as seriously as we should, more or less commit us to that particular brand of faith.

Paganism has always adopted a much greater tolerance of people's beliefs, following the old principle that we should be encouraged positively to pursue whichever faith or religion we wish without judgement. Taking part in a pagan ceremony does not prevent us from believing in the same ecumenical God as a Christian, a Jew or a Muslim. Such rites, if they follow the pagan ideal, should be truly universal.

It is not, however, always easy for us in the twenty-first century to discover how and where to draw on alternative ways of celebrating and sanctifying important moments in our lives. The ceremonies that you will find in this book come from a wide variety of sources, bringing together the rich folk traditions of both eastern and western cultures, and one of their most notable aspects is a remarkable similarity of purpose world-wide. Whether conducted by Aboriginals in Australasia, Inuits in the Arctic Circle or modern Wiccans, many of the rites enjoy a shared procedure and purpose. In terms of their scope, you may find yourself following adaptations of small rituals drawing on the fabric of traditional paganism and neo-paganism from far-flung parts of the world. Of others that seem particularly relevant or suitable, some are based on personal experience and some are borrowed from friends and acquaintances.

For people who seek a more organized ceremony, associations such as Liferites (see pages 139 and 140), established as recently as 1998, are now dedicating themselves to serving the needs of individuals who hold no formal religious beliefs and who seek to affirm their life and death in a very personal or individual manner.

Our spirituality reveals some remarkable parallels. Whether human beings lived 20,000 years ago in the bitter weather of the Ice Age, or they still exist on the edge of some dark and brooding forest, or in an inner city, they find faith in the same gods and worship before the same altars.

Marking a moment

■ The fundamental purpose of the ceremonies is to mark all aspects of life and death. In this respect they are little different from ceremonies that take place in an orthodox religious setting. But there are no laid down rules to our alternative ceremonies. They are designed for us to follow as closely or as loosely as we wish, at home or in some other quiet place. Few are intended to be solemn affairs, and the only 'guideline' is that they should be pursued honestly, truthfully and with sincerity of purpose. They exist to celebrate a birth, to mourn the passing of a loved one, to worship, to give thanks, to ask the blessing of whatever spiritual powers we care to invoke. None of them is dangerous or calls upon sinister elements, and none requires tools that are not readily and legitimately available in the countryside or the average shopping centre. All, in one way or another, are inspirational, in the sense that they provide an encouraging or exalting influence. To those of religious disposition it is a divine influence.

Sacred spaces
and sacred circles

The symbol of the circle contained within a sacred space is at the heart of many traditional rituals. Using it as a focus for positive energy, you can create such a space for healing and for personal affirmations.

It is important to define a space which becomes sacred and separate from the ordinary secular world outside. Within the space we may then create a sacred circle, somewhere the spiritual powers can be contacted safely. The oldest reasons for creating such a space include the necessity to prevent adverse or malignant influences intruding, but this does not mean that a sacred space must be permanently put aside or that there need be anything complicated about the procedure — far from it. An area of your house, garden or countryside can be sanctified very simply, to serve a particular purpose, and then can be de-consecrated immediately afterwards. It is effectively created anew in every rite.

How do I create a sacred space?
Perhaps the most important job, initially, is to do a little housekeeping by sweeping and dusting the sacred space if we are making it indoors, or clearing it of leaves and twigs if it is to be out in the open. This straightforward act establishes that we are creating a

How do I create the circle?

■ The circle does not actually have to be visible or tangible, but to mark it out rather than leaving it imaginary probably helps the participants to work out where they are. Size is not critical, though in Wicca tradition the classic circle, known as the Circle of Being, possesses a diameter of 2.7 metres (9 feet). Equally it can take in the whole area of a room or a woodland glade if so desired and does

special environment and making it as beautiful as we can. It is not to suggest that any of us is normally less than house-proud, it is more a symbolic action. We are carrying out a psychic purification, making the chosen area different from our ordinary living-space, rather than collecting dust with the vacuum cleaner! In doing this, we are sharing a similar principle with that found in more conventional faiths. Few people can have experienced stepping into a dirty church, mosque or synagogue.

Once the sacred space is set aside you will need to create a sacred circle around an altar or some other focal point. The circle is often thought of as a boundary within which to keep and concentrate power, and is usually drawn with its own small ceremony.

Purifying circles

■ However it is achieved, the periphery of the circle, once created, should then be purified. This can be done quite simply, by sprinkling it with water to which has been added a little salt.
■ The sacred circle described by a witch should not, incidentally, be confused with the circle which is used in ceremonial magic and which is drawn with a hazel wand while the magician recites pseudo-Christian rhymes.

not necessarily even have to be circular. In Wicca it is added to by a pair of outer rings so that the third circle has a diameter of 3.3 metres (11 feet), and the outline is drawn by casting the point of a ceremonial blade known as the *athame*. You can perform the same action using an outstretched arm and finger and then mark out the area of the circle with chalk, stones or twigs.

■ Sometimes a circle will exist without any help from us. It may be entirely natural – a glade in the woods or a hollow in a downland pasture. Or we may come across an ancient place of worship such as a ring of standing stones.

What tools
do I need?

For many ceremonies, though by no means all, we will need an altar within our sacred circle. Forget about sinister connotations which 'pagan altars' may bring to mind. All we are doing is providing a symbolic focus for our rite.

We can use a table, a hearth, a log of wood, a tree stump, a rock – the list is endless, although it is good to select something reasonably suitable. The top of the television or the barbecue stand are probably not among the best choices!

It is also a nice idea, when necessary, to light the altar with candles rather than electricity. Other useful ingredients to bring into the sacred space include salt, water and some kind of incense to burn in a crucible. We are including these items because they represent the four basic elements of earth, water, fire and air, which also symbolize aspects of consciousness we must be able to access.

Once the simple trappings are in place, we can rely on a number of ways to generate psychic energy. Before action, however, there must be tranquillity. Silence has often been taken as one of the most powerful means of storing spiritual energy. An initial period of quiet allows us time for meditation, to shut our eyes, relax and concentrate our thoughts on what lies ahead. Chanting also helps to detach us for a while from the material world and to step out on a spiritual pathway. We can use a *mantra*, a simple mystical sound device of which the best example is the 'OM' sound that forms a fundamental tool of Hindu and Buddhist meditation. The words we use can be made up for the occasion, but examples of suitable chants will be suggested in the course of the book.

How do I raise a psychic cone?

■ Individuals, alternately male and female, join hands and dance clockwise around the periphery of the sacred circle. The clockwise direction of the dancing is known as deosil, the converse of widdershins, and it copies the direction seen to be taken by the sun in the northern hemisphere. (South of the equator, the direction is reversed!) The circular movement can then, if desired, slowly move inward

Raising a cone of energy

Most of the rituals we perform will be carried out in order to generate psychic energy for positive use in our world. For centuries it has been widely accepted that, through the formalized 'steps' of ritual, the energy of the collective mind can be channelled as an immensely powerful tool for both good and evil. We can think of this in the shape of an upwardly directed cone which, in more orthodox religions, generally equates with the 'power of prayer'.

Many people are convinced that these psychic shapes, in which spiritual and essentially benevolent sources are raised, really do work, and they have been widely used in the Wicca movement. During the Second World War various illegal covens in Britain raised so-called cones of power in order to direct psychic forces against Adolf Hitler and prevent him invading the British Isles. Similar psychic energy is said to have been utilized by spiritual groups such as the Ethereans in the 1980s and 90s to prevent nuclear holocaust.

towards the centre, creating a spiral effect. In Wicca this is known specifically as the spiral dance. The spiral dance is always danced into the centre and out again, symbolizing a penetration into the mysteries of the other world. In effect the leader, when he or she reaches the centre, becomes the focus and transmitter of the energy that has been raised by the dance.

How do I release the energy?

■ The energy of the cone of power is directed on its way first by the participants, keeping the intent in the forefront of their minds. They are asked to visualize that which they are aiming to achieve. Then, at a given command, they must let go of the energy so that it can fly away out of the circle to its intended destination. The power is dissipated as the spiral unwinds.

Sharing or working alone?

In many parts of the world, the celebrants of alternative rites, whether called shamans, priests or some other title, prefer to work by themselves. In Europe such individuals are often known as hedgewitches, and they believe they are following the ancient tradition of the old-time village wise person.

A hedgewitch may be a man or woman, and they will practise their solitary craft for the purposes of healing and other objectives. It is, however, not at all necessary to work alone. Furthermore, collective psychic power can be a very strong tool if used correctly.

Making the ceremony a success

■ Whether an alternative ceremony is performed alone or with others, the true measure of its success or failure will depend upon what the individual gains from it. The chances of it going wrong can be substantially reduced by a small amount of forward planning and by selecting the right participants.

■ Children, in particular, will need to be introduced to the idea gradually and gently. Small children may be easily frightened by the unfamiliar, for which

reason it is good to conduct a rite among everyday surroundings. A table converted to an altar may appear foreign or intimidating, but the area in front of a hearth decked with candles and a few other objects will raise less apprehension, and involvement will seem more like play. The hearth has also stood as one of the most ancient forms of domestic sacred place. A good alternative is to conduct a ceremony in the kitchen, often the warmest, brightest and most familiar part of the house.

For most of us, the actual circumstances will dictate who and how many become involved in our alternative ceremonies. If we are asking blessings for a loved one who is ill we may choose to make our invocation quietly and by ourselves. On the other hand, should a popular member of the community die and they have asked for a non-orthodox funeral, a whole road or village may turn out for the occasion, pagans, Christians and others. It is essential, however, that the person we ask to lead a group ceremony is *bona fide* and not an impulsive volunteer who has read the books and believes that they know the routine. There are too many impostors, who may mean well but are not necessarily going to provide the best solution! Ask around or contact an organization like the Pagan Federation (see page 140). There are also some very knowledgeable and experienced Druids who may be willing to help, and a few genuine village witches still exist who understand the rituals, are deeply in tune with the changing seasons and grow their healing herbs in rambling cottage gardens.

Many of our celebrations will naturally be limited to family and friends. If we are to conduct a ceremony with a small intimate group, it is important, again, to make a sound decision on who will lead the rite. It should be someone who is recognized and respected by all the participants. I know of at least one witch high priestess who has stopped conducting alternative marriage celebrations, spoken of in Wicca as handfasting, unless the couple are personal friends of hers or long-standing acquaintances, simply because she believes that it is improper to join two people about whom she knows little or nothing.

A ceremony conducted within our own household is probably one of the nicest and most effective. It is essential, however, that all participants are comfortable with the arrangement.

Why we should
perform rituals

Ritual offers, if you like, a formal procedure that we can follow and by which we can offer our devotion. Over a period of time the manner in which ritual is enacted tends to become stylized and stereotyped, turning it into a tradition.

We can easily forget that the tradition still had to be *invented* by people just like you or me, so it is as well to take no notice of the purists who tell you that a certain ceremony must be conducted in a certain way. In her classic work *Persuasions of the Witch's Craft*, the anthropologist Tanya Luhrmann recalls a solitary practitioner named William who felt compelled to sacrifice to Zeus. One morning he drove to Silbury Hill near Avebury in Wiltshire, lit a fire at dawn and sacrificed a steak because he knew that the Greek gods had a preference for meat! No one told him how to perform his ritual, he just did as he thought best, freely and spontaneously.

According to one of the great occultists of the twentieth century, Gareth Knight, success depends on the state of mind of the ritualists, and unless they are well-trained in techniques of concentration and creative visualization, the work will prove abortive. This remark may be a little biased, and a degree of élitism is sometimes aired in magical circles. But is also true that the participants in a rite

Healing techniques

■ Many pagans practise healing, in much the same way that Christians do. The philosophy is that a person at ease, whose being is in a state of balance, is a healthy person and, by a similar token, someone who is ill is also out of balance or *dis-eased*. The healer evaluates the source of the imbalance and deals with it, whether on a physical or a spiritual level. Alternative healing techniques probably arose

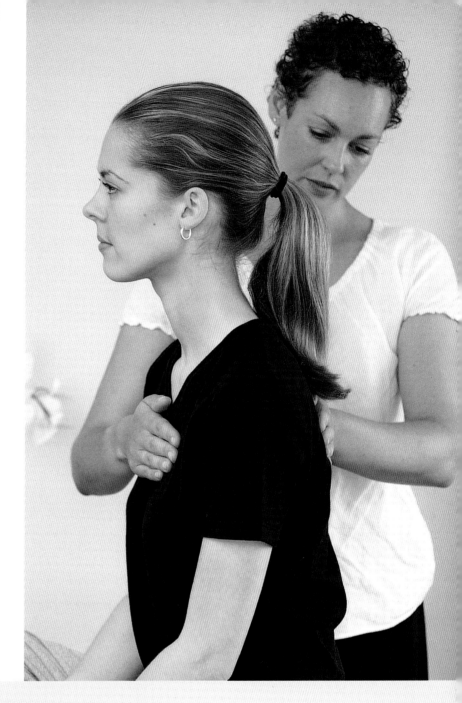

Healing encourages the rebalancing of someone who is 'dis-eased', either on a spiritual or physical level.

must be able to concentrate their minds on the purpose and to free themselves from material scepticism.

To some extent the preparation for a ritual – surroundings, use of candles rather than electric light, incense, quiet meditation – helps mental adjustment. We should also perhaps consider how we *dress* for a ceremony. There is no need for us to equip ourselves with flowing garments decked with pentagrams, stars and moons, but we should consider wearing something appropriate. We should also be prepared for a Druid or a witch, if they are invited to lead our ceremony, to arrive dressed in their ceremonial robes. These, in their way, will add a sense of importance and special occasion.

in the Far East, and one of the best known is acupuncture. We should not be attempting acupuncture without special training, but internal strengthening of the body through the stimulation of its energy channels or *chakras* was also developed in India and China and this we can learn to do with safety. We will be examining some of these healing techniques in greater detail in Chapter 6. In healing ritual, the healer may rely entirely on the power of the mind to

achieve his or her purpose. We all possess some kind of psychic ability but occasionally someone is blessed with particular gifts permitting them to act as a guide or intermediary between the spiritual powers and our human selves. Such a person is a medium, and their work of spiritual healing does not only take place in the seance room. It can be taken to the home of a sick person, to a hospice for the terminally ill or, indeed, wherever a patient needs help.

The spiritual
significance of trees

For thousands of years we have recognized that trees are imbued with a special kind of spirituality. To walk into a great forest is to walk into a living thing filled with immensity and mystery, and with depths unfathomed.

Trees are bound up with the powers of life, death and knowledge, and we are enmeshed in their mystical forces to such an extent that in Germanic and Norse religions a special tree, the World Tree or Yggdrasil, has become the focal point of this complex liaison.

When we look at a great oak in a forest glade, we can imagine its roots planted in the underworld and its uppermost branches touching the sky. Some oaks grow to a very old age – our tree may have watched over humanity for a hundred, maybe a thousand years. Trees can have an almost spectral quality: the ash extends its old and twisted limbs in a grey embrace, the fir surges upwards with calm serenity, the birch trembles in virginal shyness, the yew stands morose and dark.

Many years ago I attended a Christian midsummer service during which a bishop said something remarkable. His words have stayed with me. 'Pick out the biggest, oldest, most gnarled tree you can find and throw your arms around it, or just stand with your back pressed against it, and shut your eyes and wait. You may feel something remarkable. Something will flow out of the tree into you. It will be like energy charging a battery.' For a long time after that I had a special ash tree that stood in the centre of a remote pasture, aged, gnarled, largely finished, but with a certain undefinable aura. Once in a while I used to go to it, on my own, and do just as had been suggested. I even talked to my ash tree. Sometimes it gave me much comfort.

Wood and water

■ Water is regarded as holy because it is the essence of life itself. For this reason, in the past, the deities of pools and springs were often invoked with living sacrifices. In certain places on heights overlooking water one can still find prehistoric carvings of animals, suggesting a tradition of throwing sacrificial victims over cliffs into lakes, torrents or even the sea. The much-reported bog corpses of northern Europe, unearthed in recent times, were placed in water as part of some similar

ancient ritual and they too seem to reflect a bond between life and death. Many sacred trees also stand beside sacred pools. The Norse Yggdrasil, according to tradition, is watered by a spring that is the source of eternal and infinite wisdom, and this provides another mystical bond between trees and water.

■ In many parts of Europe springs and wells were, for thousands of years, the overseers of rites associated with the mother goddess before they were re-dedicated as Christian oratories and baptistries. Yet many people still perform little rituals which belie their true origin. We used to throw bent pins into wells as a mark of luck, following a quaint notion that anything crooked was also charmed, hence the old rhyme of the crooked man and his crooked sixpence. It is from this that the modern tradition of throwing pennies into wishing-wells has evolved.

Honouring
sacred sites

Throughout the world there exist places of ancient worship that have survived the ravages of time across centuries, if not millennia. These sacred sites are a part of our precious religious inheritance and it is important that we are able to use them for the purposes for which they were intended.

I t is also vital that we respect them, not only because of their great age and venerability but also for the benefit of future generations. In England an organization named ASLaN, standing for Ancient Sacred Landscape Network, has been established as a focus for the exchange of information about sites of spiritual importance and their care between the public, local groups and national bodies. ASLaN's pithy maxim is: 'Don't change the site; let the site change you.' The groups involved include the Pagan Federation, the National Trust, Fellowship of Isis, Druids and others including the Rollright Trust. The Rollright Stones are a group of prehistoric megalithic monuments in the Cotswolds, built from large natural boulders and first erected around 2,500–2000 BCE. In France, near the village of Carnac in Brittany, one can discover an outstanding testament to forgotten ritual. Avenues of nearly 3,000 megaliths run for hundreds of metres, a witness to an arcane belief.

Among the principal concerns must be the increasing pressure on ancient sacred sites and sharing information on creative and positive ways of management. ASLaN points out that it is not the only organization involved in this kind of activity and that Stonehenge, for example, a government-run site, can be hired out for private ceremonies. In the end, whatever we do at a sacred site must show reverence for the spirit of the place and for the nature that lives there (see page 138).

How to act

■ Essentially you should leave the place as you found it! In times of religious persecution it was a sensible precaution to leave no traces of ritual for the Church to seize upon. Ironically, in an age of greater tolerance towards spiritual belief, the same principle has become equally important for different reasons. The burgeoning popularity of stone circles and dolmens is making them intensely vulnerable. Not only does damaging archaeological remains make it harder for us, and for future generations, to understand the

history of the area, but affecting any aspect of the site will affect the spirit of the place. Graffiti daubed on ancient stones is probably the most well-publicized form of vandalism, but digging holes will damage plants and may disturb archaeological remains, while lighting fires not only destroys wildlife but also puts standing stones at risk – they can split if they get too hot. Fires can also quickly get out of hand. You may wish to leave offerings after your ceremony, but don't bury objects, and remember that even material that is biodegradable has to decay. There now tends to be a policy of barring the use of rice and paper confetti at handfastings while permitting small flowers like lavender and thyme that would occur naturally in the area. It is just as important that you don't take anything away from the site (other than litter). If you are tempted to pocket a small stone as a memento (see also page 122), remember that you may be removing something of vital archaeological importance.

CHAPTER 2

Rites
of passage

Whether we have a religious

belief or possess no clear

spiritual understanding, we

still, as human beings, find a

deep need to mark the most

important moments of our lives

with some kind of memorable

ceremony. We call these events

rites of passage.

Celebrating
the transitions of life

In this book you will come across the term 'rites of passage' – but what exactly does this mean? There are certain stages in our lives, moments of transition, during which we instinctively feel a necessity for greater guidance and protection.

If we are prepared to engage in any act of spirituality we accept, through faith, that there are forces which we cannot necessarily contact through our physical senses. Nonetheless they are recognized by way of our inner sense, our psychic perception. Whether we describe these forces as gods, goddesses or give them some other esoteric title, we have faith in their ability, at least to a certain extent, to influence and fashion our lives. It is important that we do not consider them powers to control our lives, because that would take away the independence of the human spirit to make its own moral choices and to follow its own path. One of the most familiar transitions in our lives is from waking to sleeping, and many of us brought up in the Christian faith will remember the little prayer we used to recite while kneeling by our beds: 'If I should die before I wake, I pray the Lord my soul to take...' There must be dozens of versions with similar sentiment expressed through other faiths, and what we do, in those moments before the light goes out, amounts to a small rite of passage.

In older or primitive societies, where changes such as those of puberty and menopause carry greater significance, rites of passage tend to be celebrated more extensively than in the western world. People living in tribal communities observe physical changes taking place during adolescence – hair growing on the body, breasts enlarging, voices deepening – that retain a spiritual mystery which, for us in the modern world, tends to have evaporated. For a tribesman these changes rest in the hands of spirits that he must invoke in order for the transition to take place safely and properly.

In our materialistic and technologically advanced Western society we know why these things happen and, in consequence, as the world has become more dependent on materialism and technology, our interest in celebrating rites of passage has dwindled correspondingly. Yet there are changes taking place in our material world that we cannot always regard as 'progress'. Some of them begin to cause us alarm, and there is now the glimmer of a tendency to reverse the process. In the Western world the feminist movement has begun to restore women's rites of passage and, in very recent times, those of men have received increased attention.

What are the guidelines for rites of passage?
First a sacred circle should be consecrated and provided with an altar, including any objects or materials that will be required for the ceremony (see page 18). When the participants are gathered together, they should spend a few minutes in quiet meditation. The person who is to lead should then utter a short prayer that not only invokes the spiritual powers but also identifies the purpose of the rite. Whom the individuals choose to invoke will depend upon their beliefs. The words may be a variation on the poem (opposite), which is appropriate to those ascribing to a nature-based spirituality.

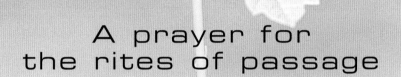

A prayer for the rites of passage

O blessed Ones,
we seek your presence here among us,
and ask that the place of this ceremony
be consecrated before you.
We have gathered here to
honour the Old and Shining,
the God and Goddess and the spirits of nature
and to perform a ritual of
[name the event].
Blessed be!

A ceremony
to mark conception

You may feel that you wish, privately, as two parents-to-be, to ask the blessing of whichever divine power you believe in, to make an invocation before the moment of conception against misfortune during the long and difficult months of pregnancy that lie ahead.

If you are asking for a successful conception, prepare your sacred circle, either indoors or in the open air, and set the altar with candles, an incense burner, some aromatic oil of your choice and a symbolic meal. The latter should include items of food that possess properties of virility and fertility. Nuts and fruits constitute the obvious choices. You may also like to include some glasses of wine or fruit juce.

You may like the idea of performing this deeply intimate rite 'skyclad' or nude, though preferably not in a public place! After some moments of meditation, call on the powers to attend your ceremony and explain to them your intention. Ask them for the boon of conception and then anoint each other with the perfumed oil. If you like this can be a preliminary to immediate love-making – the choice, as always, is yours! Either afterwards or beforehand the ritual foods should be eaten, and finally the sacred circle must be closed.

Giving thanks for conception
Once you know that a baby has been conceived you may wish to give thanks for the blessing of fertility. Again you may choose to keep this as a strictly private and intimate invocation as parents, or to invite family and close friends to join you. The sacred circle is prepared much as it was for the ceremony you performed asking for successful conception, and the altar should include oil for anointing and a symbolic feast of foods which will sustain the mother and allow her to deliver a healthy infant.

A blessing before birth

■ In the United States, Wiccans conduct a delightful ceremony to honour the expectant mother, to empower her and to establish a bond between herself and the Goddess for whom she is a channel for new life. Two large bowls are needed: one containing warm water to which an infusion of rose or lavender water has been added, the other containing dry oatmeal. Additional items include a clean hairbrush, oil of rosemary, a small floral crown, a ball of wool, a pot of herbal tea and a

towel. Those attending the ceremony may bring a small gift. Whoever is to lead the ceremony first consecrates a sacred circle and invokes the spiritual powers with a brief prayer that explains the purpose of the gathering. The leader then washes the feet of the mother-to-be in the scented water. She then transfers the feet to the bowl containing oatmeal and massages them before drying them. Someone else is directed to brush the expectant mother's hair and to groom it with the rosemary oil while she sips the herbal tea, after which the floral crown is placed in her hair. The next part of the ritual involves taking the ball of wool and passing a length around the mother's middle, knotting it to mark the girth. The ball of wool is then passed around the circle and each woman is asked to make a blessing for the baby while adding another knot. Finally the length of wool is broken off and given to the mother-to-be along with presents. The ceremony is closed by de-consecrating the circle.

Ceremonies
to celebrate birth

Since time immemorial, the two most important rites of passage have been those that oversee the beginning and ending of human life – birth and death.

At one end of the spectrum we recognize the greatest of all the eternal mysteries of our existence, the miraculous transformation of the inanimate to the animate. We witness a change from nothingness, to embryo, to foetus, to infant. Even now, at the turn of the third millennium, science can explore distant galaxies, it can send men and women to the moon and it has the means to annihilate life on our planet. But it cannot explain the simple act of magic that is birth, nor can it *create* life.

In many respects our attitudes to childbirth have become more liberal and open. In the old days childbirth was strictly women's business, even though it usually took place at home rather than in a maternity ward. It was socially regarded as a taboo subject for men, so the mother-to-be literally went into 'confinement', living out her pregnancy with a few other women kept apart from the mainstream of society. The imposition of such a primitive tradition in Europe was largely the responsibility of a Christian Church arguing that a woman who had conceived had done so 'in sin'. She could not be a part of normal society until she had been cleansed and the baby baptized to rid it of the wrongdoing in which it was born.

Thankfully we are now able to rid ourselves of such outdated behaviour and prejudice. Today, men share in the rite of passage from womb to full life. They attend antenatal clinics, practise breathing exercises and very often are present at the birth. There is also a growing tendency, once more, for a woman to have her baby at home rather than in the clinical remoteness of a hospital. This means that we are far less restricted by rules and regulations about how we celebrate the moment of birth.

Birth ceremonies

■ We have become sufficiently liberated in our attitudes to want to honour the mother for carrying her precious cargo over nine months and to revere the entry of a new human life into the world. But, there is always a faint cloud on the horizon, as despite all the modern advances in obstetrics, we should never forget that childbirth is still a risky and unpredictable business. Of course it carried much greater dangers in the past, when mortality rates among mothers and infants were frighteningly high. To a great extent this is why birth ceremonies, outside the Christian faith, have been given such a place of importance. The rites of passage that have built up around childbirth are, to some extent, designed to alleviate the anxiety created in the parents concerning the physical well-being of the mother and her baby. They are also intended to allay concerns not only among other family members such as brothers and sisters but of friends and neighbours whose lives may be affected by the arrival of a new member of the community.

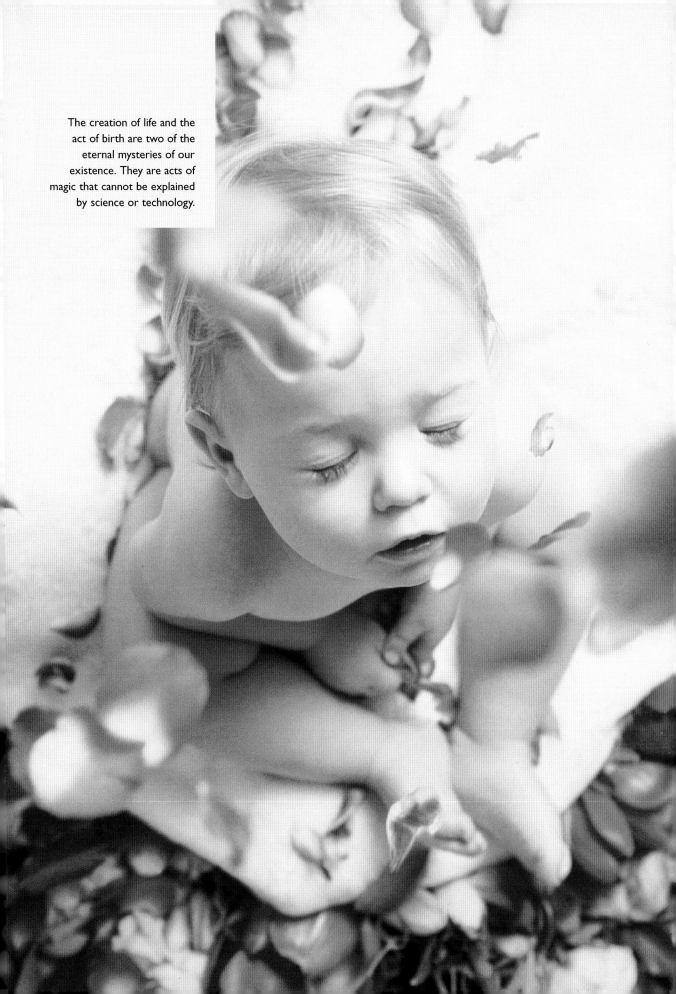

The creation of life and the act of birth are two of the eternal mysteries of our existence. They are acts of magic that cannot be explained by science or technology.

Welcoming
the new arrival

The arrival of a new baby is a time of adjustment for all the family, but any celebration should, most importantly, be at the discretion of the mother.

Both the mother and baby will be tired, whether the birth has taken place at home or in the maternity ward of the local hospital, and at first she will want to be alone with the baby's father. Liferites (see pages 139 and 140) also make the sensible point that the welcoming ceremony may best take place at home, where there is a proper freedom to conduct the ritual (hospital wards and lighted candles do not generally go together) and where the enormity of parenthood is first truly recognized.

A welcoming ceremony should include parents, grandparents, brothers and sisters and, perhaps, a few close friends. When the sacred circle is consecrated the mother and her baby enter and a prayer of thanks is offered by the leader to the spiritual power or powers the parents have chosen (see page 38). The protection of the spiritual world, in Wicca referred to as the Old Ones, is requested, to guard the child throughout its life and to give it prosperity and wisdom, health and happiness. A lovely idea is for each of those attending to have previously written a card that contains an individual blessing. The baby is then introduced to the guests one by one, and the cards can be handed to the mother along with a gift or token of that which the person wishes for the baby.

A candle or lantern can now be lit to symbolize the bright flame of new life and, if a tree has been planted for the child, it may be shown the sapling that is to grow with it over the decades to come.

Blessing a child

In Wicca a rite of blessing is performed, but it is not like a christening that frees a child from 'original sin' and commits it to a chosen spiritual path. It is suggested that a sunny day is chosen at the time of the full moon and that the ceremony is conducted out of doors. The purpose of the ceremony is to ask for the protection of the guardian spirits of the elements throughout the child's life. We should explain to the child that our lives are shared with all the other creatures and plants of the earth and that we are watched over by the Mother and Father of us all, who created the world. A blessing ceremony is as follows, as described by the hedgewitch, Rae Beth. The hands of the priest, priestess or parent are placed lightly on the child's head, and the following words (see opposite) are spoken:

A prayer for a new baby

In the names of the Triple Goddess of the Circle of Rebirth
and of the Horned God,
I now bless you and consecrate you, pagan child of the Sun and Moon.
I place you in the protection of the guardian spirits of witchdom.
To them I commend you for safe-keeping, until such time as you are old enough
to choose your own path freely.
Blessed be!

You may like to anoint the child with fragrant, non-toxic oil. Vivianne Crowley, a high priestess of Wicca, has written these accompanying words.

I anoint thy feet
Which have brought thee in our ways.
I anoint thy hands,
That they may work for what is right and true.
I anoint thy heart,
That it may beat in strength and love.
I anoint thy lips,
That they may speak no evil and give forth truth.
I anoint thy brow,
That thy mind shall seek the wisdom of enlightenment.

She then addresses the Goddess thus:

O lovely and gracious Queen of Living Light,
Thou, whose promise is that we will return after death,
To be with our own people,
And that we will know, and love,
And remember them again,
Bless this child who has returned once more to her/his own.

Saining or
naming your baby

In the Christian faith, the rite of baptism, at which a baby or a young person is named, is seen to commit them to that particular faith for the rest of their lives. Yet is this fair, when the young person may not have gained sufficient maturity or understanding to allow them to agree or disagree?

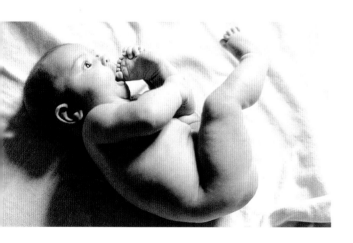

In alternative religion, naming ceremonies do not usually oblige the child to take a given spiritual direction, because it is accepted that a true and fair choice of belief can only be made later in life — and this may follow a quite different path to the faith of the parents. Generally, however, you will want to accompany the blessing of your child with a ceremony in which it is also named. In European tradition this rite, known by its Old English title of 'saining', is supposed to take place out of doors within nine days of the birth and should involve the tree that you

have planted to mark his or her birth (see page 40). The sacred circle is inscribed so as to include the tree and the guardians of the four elements are invoked (see page 18). A small intimate offering linking the child with the tree can be buried at its foot. It is also a nice idea if a vessel containing water is brought to the ceremony, so that, when the child has been anointed, the tree can also be provided with life-giving essence. In Wicca the boy or girl receives a magical name which, if the child is old enough, it will have helped to select. You are not obliged to decide on a pagan name and will give the child a name that you, as parents, have chosen.

Whoever is to lead the ceremony first explains why everyone is gathered and then asks the parents formally if they have given the matter proper consideration. Assuming that they answer in the affirmative, the naming can begin. Rae Beth suggests formally giving the child its name and greeting it with a kiss, followed by a lovely prayer that includes these words.

May the light of the Sun and the light of the Moon and stars shine on your path, that you may perceive the beauty of both the day and night. You are a child of the Mother and Father of All, beyond your human parents. Know that every end is a beginning and that the circle of creation has fulfilled itself in you . . . pagan child you are today, but that is not binding upon you. Be as your own being shall decree in future years, in joy and freedom.

In a Wicca ceremony, Vivianne Crowley indicates that the priest or the father should take the child and address the Horned God as follows. Remember, the Horned God is not the Devil or Satan, but Cernunnos, the Celtic god of nature who bears the horned head of a stag.

A naming prayer

O Horned One, Power of Sleep and Night,
Grant strength and blessing to this child.
Wrap her/him in the cloak of thy protection
And guard her/him through the journey of life.

The parents then say, jointly:

We take the oath
To raise, protect and train our daughter/son [name]
Given to us as a trust and sacred gift
By the Mother and Father of All,
Until she/he is of age
To take responsibility for her/his own life.
We will teach the ways of our Mothers and Fathers:
Love, gentleness, good example,
And firmness when called for we shall give.
Blessed be [name] and welcome to the world.

Planting a tree
for the birth of a baby

Since time immemorial the link between the life of trees and human existence has been very strong. The association is not entirely surprising, because trees are the most enduring of all living things and many of them share a similar life span to our own.

Today, in large parts of communist China, people from all walks of life are turning towards ancient folk ceremonies surrounding trees in order to share in their innate strength. The sight of the early morning callisthenics of the Mao era is being replaced by a spiritual 'wake-up' whereby people are following the popular fashion of holding, rubbing and embracing trees so that the mystical aura and strength of the tree may be transmitted. In many parts of the world the well-being of the birthday tree has been treated as an indicator of the physical and spiritual health of the person.

The relationship between child and tree

In European countries including England, France, Italy, Germany and Russia it has been a tradition to plant a tree to mark the birth of a child. The tree then becomes something of an *alter ego* and, as it grows with the child, it receives special care. If the birth-tree is felled during a person's lifetime it has been considered that the death of its human 'partner' will soon follow.

When should I plant the tree?

■ The tree should be planted as soon after the birth as is conveniently possible, and it is good if those present link hands to form a circle around the sapling. A simple invocation can then be recited, of which the Lithuanian prayer (right) is a nice example. The prayer can be modified freely to suit your particular ceremony.

Eight Favourite trees to celebrate a birth

- Oak ■ Hazel ■ Holly
- Birch ■ Pine or conifers
- Apple ■ Flowering cherry
- Bonsai

What kind of tree should I plant?

Certain trees traditionally have either masculine or feminine characteristics. Trees associated with boys have always been the resistant, rugged species like the oak and, particularly, the apple, while the more feminine trees include the willow and the birch, which has been popularly known as the 'lady of the woods'. Hazel is a good tree associated with wisdom. Trees which should *not* be planted to celebrate an infant's birth include the elder, associated with the betrayal of Jesus Christ, and the yew which is a tree of death. Rowan, blackthorn and Ash have all been strongly linked with aspects of less desirable witchcraft and are to be avoided.

In Scotland a famous oak known as the Edgewell Tree, which grows not far from Edinburgh, has been linked to the destiny of the Earls of Dalhousie. There exists a morbid legend that in July 1874, at the precise moment that Fox Maule, the 11th Earl, passed away, a massive bough from the tree crashed to the ground.

The New Zealand Maori tradition is to bury the umbilical cord beside a tree, and elsewhere in the world similar sentiments are expressed. In Papua New Guinea, for example, a pebble is rammed into the wood of the tree.

A Lithuanian prayer for trees

*That I may not fell a single
tree without holy need;
that I may not step upon
a blooming field;
that I may always plant trees.
The gods look with grace
upon those who plant
trees along roads,
in homesteads, at holy places,
at cross roads, and by houses.
If you wed, plant a wedding tree,
If a child is born, plant a tree.
If someone dies plant
a tree for their soul.
At all festivals,
during important events,
Visit trees.
Prayers will attain holiness
through trees of thanks.
So may it be!*

Birthstones
for a new-born baby

For thousands of years precious and semi-precious stones, sometimes inscribed with words or images, have been regarded as talismans, objects that confer power, of one kind or another, on to the people who wear or own them.

In ancient China the kings of the first dynasties believed that jade contained powers of immortality, and they not only wore it but regularly swallowed draughts of crushed and powdered jade, thinking that by doing so they might cheat death. Ironically the stone dust accumulating in their bodies amounted to a poison which probably hastened their demise!

In the West much of our present-day lore about birthstones is rooted in Jewish traditions found in the Old Testament. Stones identified in the book of Exodus as decorating the breastplate of Aaron, the brother of Moses, came to represent the twelve tribes of Israel. These were later adopted by Christians who gave them magical properties and then, through popular lore, identified them with the twelve apostles. It was the first-century Jewish historian Josephus who introduced the idea of associating the stones with months of the year and with signs of the zodiac as birthstones. However, the custom of wearing birthstones probably did not begin in Europe until the eighteenth century.

You may wish to give a birthstone as a present to a new-born infant, but how and in what form? It is believed by many people that the talismanic power of a stone will be increased if it is accompanied by an inscription. This can be as simple as the relevant sign of the zodiac or can include a more detailed message. By mounting the stone in a ring or some other item of jewellery, you will not only provide the means to wear the stone but also increase its potential to help its new owner.

The stones have been changed as traditions have differed down the centuries, but in modern times those most commonly associated with birth months are as follows:

Stone:	GARNET
Colour:	Wine-red or purple
Zodiac associations:	Aquarius (21 January–18 February), also Virgo
Positive influences:	Bringing humour and good health to its owner while also encouraging loyalty
Defence against bad influences:	Bad dreams and lightning
Healing powers:	Guards against a variety of ailments
Other associations:	According to folklore the garnet will change its colour in the vicinity of danger or other evil influences.

Stone:	AMETHYST
Colour:	Ranging from bluish-violet to purple
Zodiac associations:	Pisces (19 February–20 March), also Aquarius
Positive influences:	Fidelity and loyalty
Defence against bad influences:	Intemperate behaviour and rash passions
Healing powers:	Wide range
Other associations:	In antiquity amethyst was supposed to prevent inebriation in its wearer and to increase their chances of finding true love!

Stone:	JASPER (often referred to as bloodstone)
Colour:	Red, yellow, brown or dark green
Zodiac associations:	Aries (21 March–20 April), also Pisces and Leo
Positive influences:	Emotional happiness and security, sensitivity to the troubles of others
Defence against bad influences:	Easing of labour pains in childbirth; protection in a fight or war
Healing powers:	None specifically today, though once believed to cure fevers, epilepsy and to staunch bleeding
Other associations:	Jasper is used as a defence against witchcraft, Satanism and the 'evil eye'.

Stone:	SAPPHIRE (probably also lapis lazuli in ancient times)
Colour:	Blue (dark and light)
Zodiac associations:	Taurus (21 April–21 May), also Capricorn
Positive influences:	Affairs of the heart, fidelity, honesty, common sense
Defence against bad influences:	Fear and anxiety
Healing powers:	Curative value against rheumatism, jaundice and optical ailments
Other associations:	Sapphire is often associated with women. According to some Christian traditions it was the birthstone of St Paul and, from the twelfth century, was used as a gemstone in bishops' rings. It has also been widely regarded as a defence against Satanism.

AGATE

Stone:	AGATE
Colour:	Very varied but including bearded, black, eye, moss, red, tawny and tree varieties
Zodiac associations:	Gemini (22 May–21 June)
Positive influences:	Calmness and mental clarity, equilibrium of physical and emotional energy (varying according to the colour of the stone)
Defence against bad influences:	Protection against Satanism
Healing powers:	None specifically today though once believed to cure eye conditions
Other associations:	Agate is traditionally considered to be a protection against storms, fending off lightning and to assist in the location of buried treasure!

EMERALD

Stone:	EMERALD
Colour:	Green
Zodiac associations:	Cancer (22 June–22 July)
Positive influences:	Emotional fidelity and affairs of the heart
Defence against bad influences:	Protection for seafarers
Healing powers:	Mentally soothing; also of benefit to improve poor eyesight and memory and to encourage eloquence of speech
Other associations:	Emerald is often thought to give second sight or foresight.

ONYX

Stone:	ONYX
Colour:	Contrasting straight bands of variable colour, among which black and white are generally regarded as the most favourable
Zodiac associations:	Leo (22 July–23 August), also Capricorn
Positive influences:	Self-control and marital happiness
Defence against bad influences:	Cooling of excessive sexual desires
Healing powers:	Often considered to be of value in easing labour pains during childbirth
Other associations:	Black onyx has been valued as a defence against witchcraft, Satanism and the 'evil eye'. In the past it has not always been regarded favourably and has been associated with antagonism including marital stress, and with bad dreams.

CARNELIAN

Stone:	CARNELIAN
Colour:	Most popularly blood red, but also yellow and brown
Zodiac associations:	Virgo (24 August–22 September)
Positive influences:	Friendship and courage, mental clarity and physical stamina
Defence against bad influences:	Easing of labour pains in childbirth; protection in a fight or war
Healing powers:	Believed to provide a remedy for impotence and infertility
Other associations:	Carnelian was once very popular as a stone for signet rings. Red carnelian was also believed to improve menstrual disorders, bleeding gums and to heal sores.

Stone:	**CHRYSOLITE**
Colour:	Golden with a sparkling appearance
Zodiac associations:	Libra (23 September–23 October)
Positive influences:	Wisdom and good common sense
Defence against bad influences:	Protection against foolishness
Healing powers:	None
Other associations:	It was once thought that if chrysolite was engraved with the image of a donkey it would protect its wearer against gout.

Stone:	**BERYL**
Colour:	Variable, though most popularly blue–green. A pale blue form is referred to as aquamarine. It can also be a true green, golden-yellow or sometimes rose.
Zodiac associations:	Scorpio (24 October–22 November)
Positive influences:	Intelligence, hope, friendship and love, marital constancy
Defence against bad influences:	Idleness, protection for travellers, wards off Satanic and other adverse powers
Healing powers:	Believed to provide a remedy for eye complaints (green form) and jaundice (golden-yellow form), also various aches and pains
Other associations:	When engraved with the shape of a frog, beryl is considered particularly beneficial in relationships.

Stone:	**TOPAZ**
Colour:	Chiefly yellow, pink or white but also green and black
Zodiac associations:	Sagittarius (23 November–21 December)
Positive influences:	The bringer of wealth, it also offers the wearer intelligence and a proper sense of prudence
Defence against bad influences:	Mental depression, envy, danger while travelling and sudden death
Healing powers:	Believed to provide remedies for poor eyesight and heart ailments
Other associations:	In its white form topaz is extremely hard and has been treated as a 'poor man's diamond'. Its efficacy as a birthstone is said to be increased if engraved with the image of a hawk or falcon. It should not be worn by Pisceans or Virgos.

Stone:	**RUBY**
Colour:	Blood red
Zodiac associations:	Capricorn (22 December–20 January), also Cancer and Taurus
Positive influences:	Friendship and love, a woman's aid to beauty
Defence against bad influences:	Protection against lust, storms, witchcraft and Satanism
Healing powers:	Believed to provide a remedy for heart and circulatory disorders, diseases of the liver and spleen, and wounds
Other associations:	According to folklore, the ruby also changes its colour in proximity to danger or other evil influences. It is said to provide protection in battle.

Birth ceremonies
in tribal societies

Increasingly we have come to realize the importance of starting to prepare for the birth of a new baby long before it happens. We go through a range of therapeutic 'exercises' to ensure a healthy delivery. But much of this preparation is strictly practical.

If we want to find more spiritual ways of preparation we can do worse than turn to the traditions of tribal societies. In many of these cultures around the world the old ways at the time of birth are still remembered. The ceremonies are often based on ancient myths and legends, the purpose of which was to preserve and formalize certain important events and beliefs for the future.

Among tribespeople there is often a tradition that explains the miracle of the creation of life in a way people can understand. One of the more or less universal explanations of how life was created involves picturing it taking place in the mythical age of gods and goddesses. The scene is set of a 'birth spirit' who takes some clay, moulds it into the shape of a human being and then brings it to life.

The Australian Aboriginals have a marvellous story from the Dreamtime that covers the ritual of birthing in the context of two mythical figures, the black snake man and his wife, the dove. Many such stories possess an entertainment value but they also include elements of 'good practice': important guidelines that will give the mother the best chance of recovery and ensure her infant a fine healthy start in life. They are interwoven still further with strands of pure religious ritual, acknowledgement that the spirit world has given a gift of new life and that the spirits must be thanked and invoked for their consideration.

Making a baby-carrier

■ Once the baby is born it is important that it is protected from evil influences. The Dayak tribes of Indonesia make special baby-carriers from stiff, woven rattan with wood bases, and these are thought to guard not only the physical bodies but also the souls of newborn babies. The best carriers are decorated with motifs representing human figures and creatures such as tigers or dog dragons, spirits which protect the baby. They may include the faces of other

Tribal birth offerings

- nuts ■ fruit ■ a stone in a tree ■ the umbilical cord ■ the placenta

An offering to the guardian spirits

In many tribes a gift offering to the birth spirits at the time of a new arrival is considered essential, and this gift frequently takes the form of something from the actual birth process. In New Zealand, Maoris bury a piece of the umbilical cord of a new baby beside the sapling that was planted or dedicated as its birth tree. In other Aboriginal societies it is part of the placenta that serves as an offering. It is quite possible for you to copy this ceremony by asking the midwife to keep back a small part of the afterbirth or cord, securing it in a suitable container to take away and bury in the ground at the foot of your own baby's birth tree.

Birth traditions from tribal societies will often seem very strange to us and may be wholly unsuitable, but here are two (see above) from the Pacific region that you may like to copy.

benevolent deities as well as charms made from teeth and shells that are said to warn the mother of approaching danger. Less elaborate carriers are decorated with purely geometric shapes. Dayak matrons also string together beautiful netted beadwork designs which they fasten to the carriers and which are intended to invoke the guardian spirits of infants in much the same way as the motifs. The beads, mainly made of glass, offer a hard surface to repel evil.

Miscarriage
and stillbirth

Rites of passage should be available to mark every eventuality in life and this, of course, includes the sad event of death when we have to say 'goodbye' to a loved one.

At whatever stage miscarriage occurs, it marks the tragic close of a life in the making and it will be accompanied by great anguish and sorrow among the parents, grandparents and other close family members. Stillbirth is especially painful, because new life has come so far and there has been so much of a struggle by mother and baby only for that small tender flame to be extinguished at its moment of first fulfilment.

We should, of course, perform a ceremony to mark the closing of life and to provide some measure of comfort to the grieving parents. We should also give our thanks to the spirit world for giving the gift of life, however short that life may have been. There are, on the other hand, drawbacks to conducting a funeral for a baby without obtaining expert help. The spiritual views of the parents are not the only ones to be considered, and one must remember that, unlike when an older person dies, the preferences of the baby have not yet formed. One can imagine the potential for distress if the parents want a full pagan ceremony and the grandparents are staunch Christians.

It is possible to conduct your own funeral for a baby. The ceremony can be held almost anywhere providing you obtain permission, though most non-denominational funerals tend to be in a crematorium or a designated woodland burial ground (see page 68). Nor is there any established format to the service, although there will be time constraints, generally twenty minutes, at a crematorium. If the ceremony is held out of doors you will also need to consider the weather and how long you can expect people to stand at a graveside.

The best option may be to compromise, by putting the funeral in the hands of professional funeral directors and asking Liferites (see page 139), or an experienced nondenominational officiant within your own circle, to lead the rite. Then you can hold a private ceremony of remembrance at which you may choose to scatter the ashes or plant a tree in a woodland site. The tree will be dedicated to the baby to mark his or her passing, and you will be able to revisit the tree on birthdays or at the anniversary of your baby's death. If a tree was planted at the time of the baby's conception you may wish to move it to the burial site or to a place in the countryside to symbolize the freeing of the baby's spirit.

The pagan writer Starhawk has composed this moving poem (right) about the death of a baby which you may wish to read at the funeral or remembrance ceremony.

A poem for the loss of a baby

Mother of life,

Mother of death,

here is a spirit so new

that the gates of life and death

are just an archway in her dancing ground.

She has danced her way back to you.

Her passage is easy

but mine is hard.

I wanted to hold her living flesh

and feel her soft breath and her heartbeat.

(I nurtured her in my body;

I would have fed her from my breasts.)

I would have cared for her

and watched her first steps

and listened for her voice.

No other child that may come to me

will ever be what she would have been.

Nothing, nobody, will ever replace her.

Whatever healing I may find,

this loss will always be a part of me.

(Bless my womb, which has the power

to create life and death.)

Bless my arms

that would have embraced her.

Bless my hands that would have lifted her.

Bless my heart that grieves.

Starhawk

Later rites
of passage - puberty

During our adult lives we go through at least two significant changes which, in the past, have been far more commonly welcomed by rites of passage than is customary today.

These changes, at puberty and menopause, mark the beginning and ending of our ability to procreate. The first is a rite that honours growing up for both sexes, the often perplexing and awkward transition from child to young adult. Unquestionably the most important rule when considering how best to mark puberty in our children is to follow their wishes. Many modern teenagers will run a mile at the thought of being put through what they perceive as the thoroughly embarrassing ordeal of a ritual to celebrate the voice breaking, hair appearing on different bits of the body, breasts requiring support and, horror of horrors, advertisement of first periods! If, however, your son or daughter likes the idea of a ceremony when the objective has been explained to them quietly and privately, a simple rite may actually help them through this first major passage after their birth.

A ceremony for a girl's first menstruation

The change to young womanhood can be a particularly frightening business. Menstruation is often poorly explained and may not be properly understood as something to be proud of, a time of transition to the grown-up world – even if, as so often happens these days, it takes place at the age of nine or ten.

Vivianne Crowley has described to me a lovely ceremony performed in the Toronto region of Canada. A girl, who has experienced her first period during the warmer summer months is escorted by her family to a beautiful lakeside. She is dressed in a white gown and carries flowers in her hair. After she has been blessed

Marking manhood

■ Something similar to the ceremony that Vivianne described, though a little more macho, can be arranged for a boy, as he enters manhood for the first time. The idea of ritual circumcision and ordeals to prove his toughness were once very much a part of tribal custom for a boy, and they gave him a respect that was absent during his childhood. No one is suggesting copying such ceremonies, but a symbolic gesture towards his new-found importance is still appropriate. Small gifts

Moon huts

■ The American writer on paganism Margot Adler points out that a number of women are now using so-called 'moon huts' during menstruation. These are retreats from worldly life which, it is claimed, were created in ancient tribal societies by women in order to celebrate the mysteries of womanhood and to provide times for collective exchange.

and the spirits have been invoked to give her a long and fruitful adult life, she enters the water, accompanied by the person who leads the ceremony, and immerses herself, allowing the white robe to float away from her. While discreetly hidden by the water, she is helped to don another robe, this one coloured red. Having entered the lake in the white innocence of childhood, she leaves it clothed in the symbol of her newly found adulthood. The ceremony can easily be performed, as an alternative, from a quiet seashore or in a swimming-pool out of public hours.

associated with manhood can be presented by family and friends. A key to the house is one obvious example. This can form part of a simple ceremony giving thanks to the God and Goddess for his safe growing up and asking their blessings on a long, healthy and happy life. Boys may, however, be far more reticent than girls about participating in ceremonies of this kind, and it is important that the occasion takes place with their full agreement.

Celebrating
the menopause

Most of us, if we are strictly honest, dread the process of ageing and we see it as a personal foretaste of death. If we are to abandon a spiritual belief, it is most likely to occur in middle age.

These days we live in a society focused securely on youth and obsessed negatively with ageism, as is demonstrated in a market place where, beyond the age of fifty, we are increasingly unable to secure work. What do we do in response? We try to disguise the natural process of ageing by dyeing our hair and, if resources allow, indulging in plastic surgery

to obtain face-lifts and tummy-tucks. Women are increasingly encouraged to resort to hormone replacement therapy (HRT) with its various pros and cons.

Many hundreds of years ago, however, the time in her life at which a woman began the often drawn-out process of 'the change' was an occasion of true celebration. As a mother she had, after all, brought her own children into the world and raised them to adulthood. She had acquired the status of a matriarch imbued with great experience of the joys and hardships of life. A woman entering the menopause was one to whom others could turn as a source of mature wisdom, a grandmother at whose knee advice and comfort could be sought. In the twenty-first century, women in their forties and fifties are finding new expression and meaning for their lives as children leave home and responsibility for the care and upbringing of others diminishes. They are returning to careers and discovering different kinds of spiritual fulfilment. For many, the onset of menopause coincides with a fresh and exciting 'age' of womanhood.

If she is to follow the outlines of a pagan nature-based ceremony, she will arrange for a priestess to open the rite by drawing and purifying a sacred circle, followed by a request to the guardians of the quarters and the Goddess and God to attend. The priestess will ask for their blessing on the occasion and guide the woman in giving thanks for a fruitful life. She may also feel it appropriate to make promises about what the coming years will mean in terms of new responsibilities and objectives. The priestess will then ask the deities to witness the rite of passage from one stage to another.

Rather as the girl passing with her first menstruation from childhood to young childbearing womanhood

changed her dress from white to red, so the woman leaving this fertile stage of her life may also wish to begin the ceremony in a red dress and leave it having changed into another colour of her choice.

There is no reason why a similar rite cannot be performed for a man entering the status of an elder, though, for him, the time of transition will be less clearly defined. It could, perhaps, take place on his fiftieth, fifty-fifth or sixtieth birthday, depending on when and how his lifestyle changes from that of a young man to one of seniority.

Liferites

■ The Liferites organization (see pages 139 and 140) has done much to pioneer a restoration of the celebrations that once accompanied cessation of the ability to procreate. They suggest that an appropriate rite of passage should take place a year and a day after the last period has ended, by which time a woman can be reasonably certain of menopause. The woman may choose to gather exclusively female friends about her or to have all her family, including men, around her.

CHAPTER 3

Ceremonies to
mark death
and rebirth

The transition from death to

another life requires a very

important rite of passage. Since

time immemorial the human mind

has been conditioned to the belief

in an another world where the soul

will travel, either to reside in a

spiritual eternity or to rest as part

of a cycle of death and rebirth.

Egyptian rituals
of the dead

The ancient Egyptians held the paradoxical view that while the soul was led 'naked' through the stages of judgement towards paradise or obliteration, any Egyptian who could afford to do so should be interred with all the human requirements that he would need in the next world.

The pharaohs, of course, took rites of death to extremes when they built the Pyramids and surrounded their remains with all the luxuries they had known in life. It was because of the belief that the body might be restored in heaven that the Egyptian who could afford the process had his earthly remains preserved as a mummy. The process of transition was envisaged in the most minute detail and, in order to follow the 'correct procedures' and achieve unity with the gods, the priests of ancient Egypt prepared a complicated series of spells. Known as *The Book of the Dead*, these were inscribed on the interior walls of coffins and sarcophagi belonging to pharaohs and others of noble birth. Instructions for the handling of the corpse were also very precise, and such was the confidence in a further existence that one of the important rituals was the opening of the mouth so that it might breathe again.

The ancient Egyptian felt no anxiety towards death because the soul, as he or she walked up the pathway towards the heavenly light, followed the route first taken by Osiris, the god of the dead, through whom there was a bright awakening and a rebirth. Even the poor who could not afford mummification believed that those given the proper rites still had the opportunity to journey through the gates of the netherworld and live with Osiris in eternity. The Egyptians recognized that Osiris had once lived as a great king who had suffered a violent death. He had been restored to live eternally in the other world because the gods and goddesses had collected the parts of his shattered body and observed special magical rites over them. The logic proceeded that every man and woman would live for ever if friends and relatives did for the body of the deceased what the deities had first done for Osiris.

Funeral rites in ancient Egypt lasted for eighteen days. The dead person was interred with all the riches that could be provided and was often accompanied by an image of Osiris made up of painted cloth filled with barley. Some kind of fluid was then added so that the grain would sprout in a symbolic regenesis of life within the tomb.

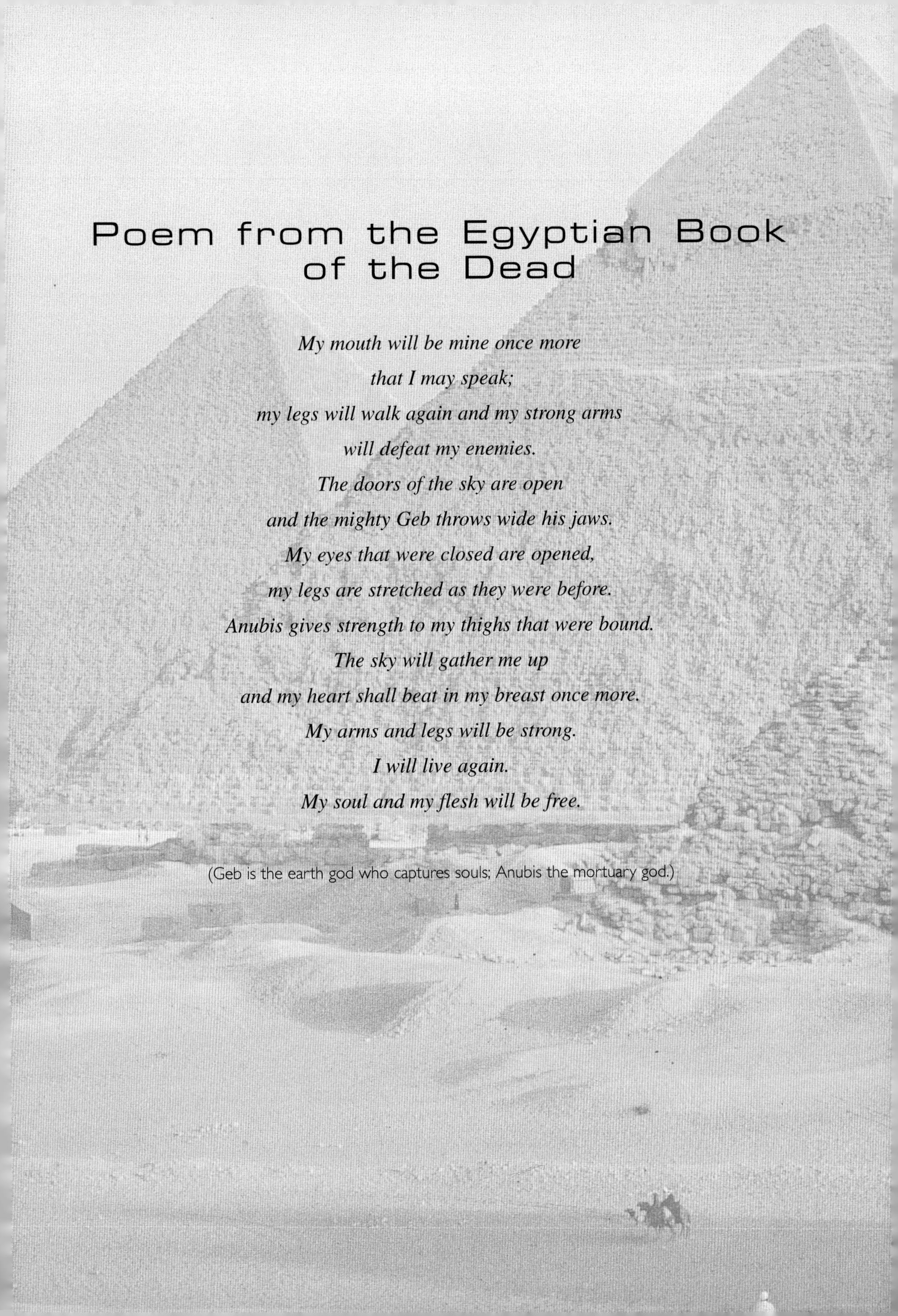

Poem from the Egyptian Book of the Dead

My mouth will be mine once more

that I may speak;

my legs will walk again and my strong arms

will defeat my enemies.

The doors of the sky are open

and the mighty Geb throws wide his jaws.

My eyes that were closed are opened,

my legs are stretched as they were before.

Anubis gives strength to my thighs that were bound.

The sky will gather me up

and my heart shall beat in my breast once more.

My arms and legs will be strong.

I will live again.

My soul and my flesh will be free.

(Geb is the earth god who captures souls; Anubis the mortuary god.)

Native American
rites for the dead

The ceremonies for the dead have varied considerably among Native American tribes, though, as in so many other cultures, the need for a rite of passage and the belief that the dead person is setting out on a long and difficult journey is universal.

There is a common belief that the body passes to a land of ghosts where it is given with 'spirit food' as a kind of communion, after which it may never return to the land of the living.

As far north as the home of the Aleut and Inuit tribes close to the Arctic Circle, burial is probably the most widespread convention and it has taken place either in the earth, under mounds or in caves. The Great Lakes tribes such as the Huron and the Iroquois often preferred to leave the bodies on raised platforms, where the elements decayed them naturally. Afterwards the bones were gathered up and deposited with solemn ritual in the common tribal burial ground.

In many areas, both in the plains and the mountains, trees were also used as natural platforms and, northward from the Columbia river, particularly among the Chinook, the body was buried in a canoe that was then raised upon posts. The Nanticoke and Choctaw scraped the flesh from the bones, which were then wrapped in a bundle and kept in a box in the home. In the arid regions farther to the west and south-west, cremation tended to be the rule.

The burial ceremony usually included the placing of useful articles in the grave for the journey of the dead person. These generally included food and, for men, weapons of war and hunting, while women were

accompanied by household items and pretty dresses. These items, however, were often smashed or ripped to pieces because it was believed that unless they were mutilated or 'killed' their astral forms would not accompany the dead person. The mourners performed a solemn dance in which the relatives cut themselves and blackened their faces before going their separate ways to grieve in solitude. This might include ritual wailing and could continue, morning and evening, sometimes for weeks.

Amongst the earliest evidence of funeral rites amongst North American Indians are the mysterious earth mounds found in the Mississippi Basin and the Gulf States. Inside one of these extraordinary structures no less than six hundred hatchet blades were discovered. In another, hundreds of ornaments fashioned in copper and silver had been deposited. Some contained skulls filled with cremation ashes, in others whole bodies had been interred lying flat or doubled up. The beliefs and identity of those who built them remains a fascinating enigma.

Among Native American tribes there tends to be a universal fear of mentioning the name of the deceased, since to do so is believed to bring ill-luck. The bereaved family sometimes went to the lengths of adopting another name to use as a substitute! It has also been a common practice to destroy the property of the dead, even to the killing of their horse or dog. Again this has been in line partly with the notion that effects, living or inanimate, cannot accompany the deceased to the other world unless their physical form is changed. In addition it has reflected a fear that the ghost of the dead person might be encouraged to remain in the vicinity in order to be with his or her earthly belongings.

There also exists a shared belief, by no means restricted to Native Americans, that the ghost of the dead person is very vulnerable. Among the Inuit of Alaska, there has been an old custom that when someone dies in a village all work ceases. The relatives of the dead person have actually been obliged to give up work for three days afterwards. It is taboo during that time to use any instrument with a cutting edge such as a knife or an axe, or anything sharp-pointed like a sewing needle. This ruling is made out of concern that the invisible ghost, still wandering around the village, might accidentally be cut or stabbed.

Polynesian and
Eastern funeral traditions

Much of the old ritual of the Polynesian Pacific islands has been lost as a result of Christian evangelism. In the late 1800s, however, William Wyatt Gill recorded some of these traditions and they were published in a collection, South Pacific Myths and Songs.

The death rites of the Polynesians and the laments sung at the funeral of a loved one are very beautiful. According to custom, on some of the islands the ceremonies lasted up to a fortnight. The mourners used to blacken their faces, gash themselves with shark's teeth, and wear russet-coloured fern leaves in their hair as part of the ritual. They would also dip their loincloths into putrefying mud to symbolize the decay of death. On the day of the funeral, laments and dances composed in honour of the dead person were performed and some sign of their return would be sought over the ocean, first to the north, then the west, followed by the south and east.

At the graveside, five coconuts were cracked open and the juice poured out on the ground to symbolize life returning to the earth from whence it came. The shells were then wrapped in leaves and cloth and tossed into the grave one by one, with other food, accompanied by the words: 'Eat the food we bring to thee, O loved one!' When the fifth parcel was dropped the mourners uttered the words: 'Farewell, we remain with thee no more.'

You may feel that you can adapt these traditions. The wearing of red or russet, the colours of autumn, is a beautiful idea, and a muffled drum can be beaten, slowly, to accompany the words of farewell. The chant (right) is an adaptation of one of the Polynesian chants recorded by William Wyatt Gill from the island of Mangaia.

Many Eastern tribal cultures have been governed by interesting taboos such as those based on a widespread belief that the soul can be removed from the body forcibly. In Burma, the Karen people used to tie their children to part of the hut with a sacred rope when a funeral cortège was passing by, lest their spirits should be lured away into the corpse. At the graveside, bamboo poles carried by each mourner were lowered into the open grave to show his or her soul, should it accidentally fall in, the safest way to climb out.

Similar taboos are associated with other Oriental funerals. Superstition requires that when the lid is about to be placed on the coffin in the house, the mourners step back several paces or even move into another room because a person's health is believed to be placed at risk if their shadow is interred inside the coffin. When the coffin is about to be lowered into the grave, all but the next of kin step back a few paces for the same reason.

Much of south-east Asia is strongly influenced by Buddhism, in which death is seen as a gateway to reincarnation, part of the endless cycle of rebirth or *Samsara*. Death offers no respite because the deeds of the life that is over will affect the quality of lives in the future until the ultimate *nirvana* is reached, the eradication of all things which tie us to the cycle of rebirth.

A Polynesian chant

Here we are gathered, toward the setting sun.

Tarry with us this evening before you travel far away

By a perilous path to the spirit land.

Halt on your journey and turn your eyes back toward us.

Look again upon those who loved you

And whose days are spent in tears.

Rest as you journey toward the setting sun where your home is.

Encircled with the red leaves of mourning, we grieve for you.

The drum of death is beating.

Weeping, we would follow you, yet you go far away

By a perilous path to the spirit land.

Rush forth O guardian winds

And bear our loved one gently on his/her way.

We weep for thee and desolate is our home.

Guided by the Goddess you shall safely reach your home

Gliding over the shimmering sea

To rest beneath the glowing tide.

Chinese and
Japanese funeral rites

Before a traditional Japanese funeral, a small table is placed in an alcove of the house. This follows the belief that there is a special place in the house, conventionally a recess or alcove, where the soul of the dead person is believed to rest.

The table is covered with a white cloth on to which are placed, from left to right, a flower, incense and a lighted candle. The table also contains a bowl of rice and some water. All these things are offerings to the departed soul.

If the dead person is kept at home, the head is turned towards the north, the direction of *nirvana* or paradise. He or she is washed and clothed with garments that resemble an old-fashioned travelling outfit. This includes a purse, into which six pieces of money are placed to pay the ferryman to cross the river of death. This outfit is called Shinishozoku, a dress for a journey to eternity. Outside the house a small notice of mourning and a lantern are hung.

The important role of the mourners

In the old days, all the people attending a Japanese funeral wore white, but more recently the convention has been to fall-in with the rest of the world and dress in black. After cremation, a meal is eaten at the crematorium and the person's ashes are collected. In Japanese ceremony chopsticks are not just for eating food and a special etiquette is attached to them. The fragments of bone are picked out using the chopsticks and passed from person to person, then the urn is taken home to be placed in an alcove for thirty-five days. As they return to the house each of the mourners is sprinkled with salt to exorcize them and some money is given to the family of the deceased. The mourners receive a smaller gift in return. After the funeral, memorial or remembrance ceremonies are no less important because the Japanese believe that the spirits of the dead come to see us when we hold these rites.

A Chinese funeral lasts somewhat longer: over forty-nine days, of which the first seven are the most important, according to one tradition, and over a hundred days according to another. At the time of the funeral, the world-wide sense of a journey prevails.

The soul of the deceased must be provided with all the necessities for travel and with proper insurance against the influence of evil spirits. Mourners bring gifts of food and money as well as paper models which

represent all the requirements that the dead person may need in the other world – a beautiful house, an expensive car and so on – often vastly exceeding anything he or she experienced or expected in life. Gifts are also brought to appease any adverse spirits that may be present. All these things are burned in the sacrificial incense crucible.

In Taoist belief the soul of the departed relative becomes divided at death: one part rises to heaven, one remains in the grave where it is entitled to receive offerings from the living, while a third inhabits the ancestral shrine kept at the home of the eldest male heir. Remembrance prayers are said every seven or ten days so that the dead person is better able to take a favourable rebirth.

Other burial rites

■ In the West we tend to bury or scatter ashes in one place, but a Far Eastern tradition, based on Buddhist belief, includes Bunkotsu, the placing of the ashes in several different spots, following the idea that when the Buddha entered nirvana his ashes were buried at eight different places. In Egyptian religion it was also sometimes the practice to scatter remains in more than one place following the belief that the parts of the God, Osiris, were interred all over Egypt.

Tailoring to
the individual

For many pagans death is inextricably linked with rebirth. It is symbolized in the Wicca spiral dance and in the silken cord that binds the physical and the spiritual worlds.

A t the moment of death the cord is severed and our immortal self is free to wind its way inwards and back, following the path of the spiral, to the source of all life and death, the *Ewigweib*, the Great Mother. We greet her, face to face, for the first time. In her arms we are rejuvenated and transfigured before she points us towards the spiral path again, this time outwards and upwards towards the struggle of rebirth.

Contact the close friends of the person who has died and arrange to meet them at one of his or her favourite places in the countryside or at someone's home. Choose things from the person's life that you know gave them particular pleasure, perhaps a favourite poem and some of their favourite music. In advance ask those who knew them well to prepare small individual eulogies that recall good things about them and that can be read out during the ceremony. The enduring spirit that has moved gently on to another place may be envisaged as a flame in the darkness, and you may feel it appropriate for everyone to light a candle symbolizing this spark of eternity. As each person says something about their friend the other members of the group should be asked quietly to visualize the one who has left us behind. There is nothing wrong in combining parts of the Christian canon, or that of any other 'orthodox' religion with pagan material. During its requiems at least one pagan

group in the United States draws on the beautiful and greatly moving words of the *Book of Ecclesiastes* (12. 6) altering the word God to Goddess.

Or ever the silver cord be loosed or the golden bowl be broken, or the pitcher be broken at the fountain, or the wheel broken at the cistern.
Then shall the dust return to the earth as it was, and the spirit shall return unto the Goddess who gave it.

Our remembrance ceremony may be an appropriate moment to plant a tree, in celebration of life, but this planting should be of a yew, the ancient tree of death, sacred to the goddess Hecate who guards the pathways of the night. At the end, those who have joined in should share cakes and wine in their friend's honour.

How should I arrange a remembrance ceremony?

■ One does not need to be a pagan to give a relative or friend a non-denominational funeral. When my mother died in 1999 she was cremated in Bath, Somerset, and the ceremony was led by a sympathetic Methodist clergyman. Although she believed that God was the Christian one represented in the Holy Bible, she also nurtured a profound mistrust of the 'Church Establishment'. So the short

service that we agreed on included a minimum of Christian dogma and rhetoric, instead it was a fond reminiscence of her life with tapes of her favourite music played – the Adagietto from Mahler's Symphony No. 5, the 'Laudate Dominum' from Mozart's *Solemn Vespers* and Brahms' 'Alto Rhapsody'. Afterwards we took her ashes away to scatter in a tranquil place she had enjoyed during her latter years.

Woodland and
personalized burials

Should you decide that you intend to go ahead and perform a pagan or non-denominational funeral without professional assistance, there is a lot of administrative detail that you will need to arrange first.

In most countries, there are rules and regulations about procedures when someone dies (see also page 48), and government publications are often available to explain what you should do. The Liferites organization (see pages 139 and 140) also produces a series of excellent pamphlets to guide you through the process from when death occurs to the actual funeral.

What is a woodland burial?

Many people are attracted to the idea of being laid to rest beneath a tree in a woodland setting. Essentially

woodland funerals are ecologically friendly or 'green', and many local authorities in the UK and the USA have now established woodland burial sites. The person is buried on land that is suitably managed in order to make it attractive to wildlife while allowing for the development of sustainable flora. In many such sites, instead of marking the grave with a headstone, a tree is planted with the idea that, over the years, the site will become a woodland. If your local authority has not established such a place, they may still allow you to purchase a plot for the purpose, though it will be more costly to buy.

Scattering the ashes

When someone is cremated and their ashes are placed in the Garden of Remembrance, they cannot usually be scattered on the surface. With the present-day pressures on crematoria, the gardens would very soon become knee-deep in our mortal remains. The policy is to place the ashes, in their container, in a communal burial plot and to mark the place with a small remembrance stone that includes an identification number. This, however, may not suit everyone, and there will be some who, for whatever reason, wish their ashes to be scattered freely in a favourite place.

There is no law against this, but a certain amount of discretion may be needed. If you propose to carry out the scattering on privately owned land, and in the UK for example that includes Forest Enterprise, National Trust and National Park property, while in Europe it involves more or less all open land, technically you should ask permission. A person's ashes, however, take up very little space. The crematorium will give you a casket or a small cardboard box containing a polythene bag tied with string. Inside, the ashes are of a uniform colour with the texture of small granules, so they are in no sense unpleasant to handle and are totally hygienic. Tact is the key. My suggestion is that you select the spot where you wish to scatter the ashes, whether it be a wood, a stream, an open meadow or the seashore. Choose a day when there are not crowds of people to gawp at your ceremony.

One small practical point, without wishing irreverence: do check which way the wind is blowing and make sure that everyone present is upwind of the scattering otherwise they may come into closer contact with the deceased than they had intended.

What coffin should I choose?

■ It is generally recommended to avoid using hardwood coffins because of the length of time they take to biodegrade. Cardboard may, on first consideration, seem a poor alternative, but such coffins are made carefully and tastefully. The most important thing to remember is not to get cardboard coffins damp beforehand! Other options include a wicker coffin or perhaps a wicker platform on which the body is laid, wrapped in a shroud.

Ancient
sacred sites

Some years ago, while in Ireland, I climbed the sacred hill of Tara on a wet and windy day to stand alone amid the weathered stones of a circle that still remembers the ancient gods of the Celts.

The magnetism of the immediate surroundings and the provocative view out across the misty landscape of Eire gave me, I like to think, some inkling of the aura that the place must have held for those Celtic worshippers of yesteryear. Tara retains a tremendous ethos, a character that it shares with many other sacred sites. On remote Scottish islands I have walked for miles over moorland that seems to have been untrodden for centuries to brush my fingers over standing stones, raised in supplication to the sky like weathered grey hands, and I have sensed the same spiritual strength that one can feel emanating from ancient trees. In the Dordogne region of south-west France you will find caverns that were sanctuaries of the distant Ice Age, full of images which illustrate the most extraordinary demonstration of human faith in the supernatural.

The allure of ancient monuments
Age-old sites are places of time-honoured worship, and today they can provide us with immensely powerful

Stone circles

■ Ancient places of worship can be discovered all over the British Isles and Europe. Many of them can be located through checking Ordnance Survey maps. In the United Kingdom, Dartmoor and the Western Isles of Scotland provide a treasure trove of stone circles and monuments.

settings if we care to seek them out for our alternative ceremonies. Some of the better-known ancient monuments, such as Stonehenge in Wiltshire, are now restricted for such personal events because of their burgeoning popularity, which, coupled with the mindless vandalism of the few, has begun to threaten their very existence. Similar restrictions apply to some sacred Indian sites in the United States. It is, however, still possible to reserve some of them under supervision, and there are numerous less well-publicized sacred places, of equal spiritual significance, to which we can gain free access, providing that we respect them as sanctuaries, avoid defacing them in any way and leave them as we find them.

Sanctuaries in times gone by were often not only constructed 'in the round' but also placed as close as possible to the sky. Nomadic societies that tend not to build enduring structures from wood or stone rely simply on high vantage points such as hills and mountain tops to provide locations for their hallowed grounds. Often these are places where the spirits of ancestors are believed to live. In the Old Testament such shrines are simply referred to as 'high places'. All observe the principle of getting closer to the spirit world, so often imagined to be in the sky.

By the same token, holy places are often built as tall as possible. This is ably demonstrated in the Egyptian pyramids or the spires and towers of Christian churches. Sometimes in the ancient world sanctuaries such as ziggurats, of which the biblical Tower of Babel, described in the Old Testament *Book of Genesis* (11.1–9) is probably the most famous, were actually constructed with sloping ramps running from top to bottom in order to provide a stairway for gods and goddesses to descend and ascend.

We can do worse than follow these ancient examples. When my mother died, I was faced with a decision about where to scatter her ashes. She did not wish her mortal remains to be buried in a casket, now the norm in many Gardens of Remembrance following a cremation, so my son and I climbed to one of the highest points on the South Downs, where she had spent her later years. On a cold but sunny and otherwise perfect day, encompassed by a view of breathtaking beauty and close by where my father lies, we let the winter wind take her in its arms.

CHAPTER 4

Ceremonies
to honour the
cycle of nature

Alone with rocks and sky, sea and

rivers, plants and animals, the

natural world becomes part of

a common frame – strong, self-

sufficient and at one with itself.

Our eyes are opened and we see

clearly the spiritual strength in

the immovability of a mountain,

in a brilliant shaft of light, in the

indomitable resilience of a tree,

in the power of a volcano.

Ceremonies
of the natural world

Despite our cosy existence, insulated by twenty-first-century technology, the most worldly of souls among us can still find ourselves in awe of the forces of nature.

A mighty storm, a prolonged drought, a massively rising flood tide – these events can bring a feeling of primal dismay to our hearts. We become conscious of the anger of the elements and our senses open, just for a while, to the awareness that there are controlling spiritual forces behind such events.

One of our problems in the modern world is that a lifestyle of computer chips, fast food and television soaps has eroded our old faith in the spiritual mysteries. They have been lost, piece by piece, down the arches of the years as we have drifted from the magical and the mystical towards a reverence for more prosaic gods. Only the thinnest of memories is left, rooted deeply in the recesses of our minds to bubble up now and again. When our cosseted existence becomes threatened and when technology seems able to offer no security, there comes a conviction about things which lie wholly beyond that which we can see and feel and touch through our ordinary physical senses.

We have grown apart from the gods of earth and sky, yet if we step outside our technological cocoon and retreat into the elements of the natural world, our perceptions begin to change. These elements are the physical extremities of a greater unseen potency and we, the human intruders, suddenly realize that we are bound by the claustrophobic prison of our own physical frailty and our mental limitations.

The age of the great pagan cults that focused so much attention on the living world seems long ago. The

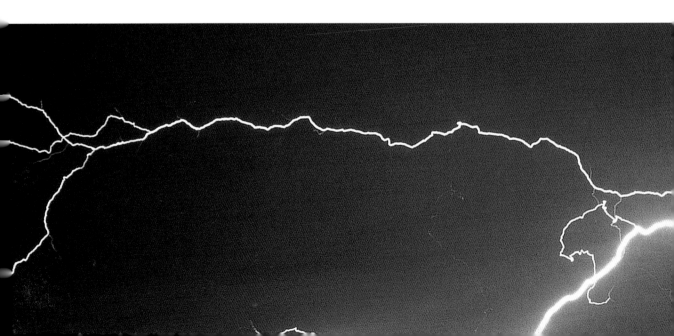

To witness the immensity
of natural forces in the world
around us is to understand
something of the faith our
forebears had in the gods
of the earth.

founding fathers who laid the blueprint for the native religions were the prehistoric hunters of the Ice Age. These distant ancestors experienced the same restrictions, but as a way of life. Living hand-in-glove with nature, their life depending on the caprices of the elements, they believed passionately in the spirituality of its forces. They placed their faith in two antagonistic yet sexually charged champions.

The unpredictable male god whose first tangible painted images, those of the dancing horned spirit, are to be found in the Ice Age caverns of western Europe and who, in later millennia, the Celts worshipped as Cernunnos stands facing the great Goddess. In her rests all the femaleness of the living world. She is the antithesis of the horned god, yet through this frenetic spirit she conceives her harvest. We have known her by many names. The ancient Egyptians called her Isis. She was Ishtar to the Babylonians, Nerthus to the people of the Celtic Bronze Age, the Artemis of Ephesus, Diana to the Romans, Freya to the Vikings. She is, as she always has been, the mistress of the moon and stars above, the timeless and ageless essence of Mother Earth below.

We may have lost our intimate contact with the spiritual powers of the natural world but this does not mean that they have gone away! If we reach out strongly enough and far enough, they may be willing to listen to us. This chapter is focused on the cycle of nature and how we may address its spirituality.

Celebrating
the spring

One of the oldest but also the simplest of ceremonies to mark Beltane is to light a bonfire or Belfire! If you live in a town apartment with no access to a garden, light a big candle instead.

In days gone by, bonfires were lit on hilltops to honour the divinities bringing life and fertility back to the world with their heat and light as well as purcation, and people used to jump over the fire for blessings. A maiden or youth might do so to increase his or her chances of finding a spouse. A woman would make the leap to ensure that she became pregnant or to rid herself of the curse of barrenness. Jumping the bonfire or candle is something we can all do, provided we wear sensible clothes that are not going to catch alight and that the fire is small and not blazing too vigorously.

The Belfire should be lit at midday, and a variation on the single Belfire is to light two a short distance apart. Bring to the ceremony something from the old year that you no longer need and can be discarded. Then run between the fires and throw it away while asking for blessings on your life through the coming months of summer.

The Maypole

The best known of the May Day celebrations is dancing around the maypole, once erected throughout Europe with all its phallic symbolism. We can either join in village celebrations involving a communal maypole, or we can build our own to whatever size will fit our back garden, our town balcony or our kitchen floor! You will need to obtain a wooden pole that can either be anchored firmly in a bucket of sand or a wooden base, or dug into the earth. A tall rough-cut fencing post will do nicely if you have no facility to go out and find (with permission) a suitable young trunk in the countryside. There are many traditional May songs but that from Padstow in Cornwall is a particularly good one (see right).

The hawthorn

■ Paddy Slade describes how each person attending the may tree should bring with them about twenty metres of coloured ribbon. Each length is then attached to the trunk of the hawthorn, and the celebrants perform the weaving dance, each holding his or her end of ribbon. Men turn left and dance clockwise while women dance in the opposite direction. The idea is to plait the trunk to symbolize the binding of summer warmth and growth into the tree.

A cle...
mi...

I celebr...

A...
And t...
Now is t...

Burn ...

A song for May

Unite and unite and let us all unite
For Summer is a-come in today.
And whither we are going we all will unite
In the merry morning of May.

With the merry ring, adieu the merry Spring
For Summer is a-come in today.
How happy is the little bird that merrily doth sing
In the merry morning of May.

The young men of Padstow they might if they would
For Summer is a-come in today.
How happy is the little bird that merrily doth sing
In the merry morning of May.

The young women of Padstow they might if they would
For Summer is a-come in today.
They might have made a garland with the white rose and the red
In the merry morning of May.

Cerei

cele

Druids famously celebra

day of the year, 21 June,

Bronze Age monument of

Wiltshire, England. At mi

eve of the Solstice, a sile

place, followed by the da

I t begins impressively as a
trumpet blows a welcoming
winds and reaches its climax
above the horizon. Many witches
Litha, heavy with sexual connotati
God is at the peak of his powers
him welcome. If you have any i
your ceremonies naked or 'skycla

This has long been an occasion
dark in honour of the burning, sl
and two elements, fire and w
because the Solstice is a time fo
the old while revitalizing the new.
that you associate with problem
throw it into the fire. The eve is
and there is a Celtic tradition of
gorse in order to burn out evil spi
countries sprigs of gorse are place

Revellers in the past used to ca
called *cressets* when they wandere
another, and they would be ac
dancers, a hobby horse, a drag

A simple

wedding ceremony

The high priestess Caroline Wise has provided the basis for this version of a non-denominational marriage that we can all use and adapt as we wish.

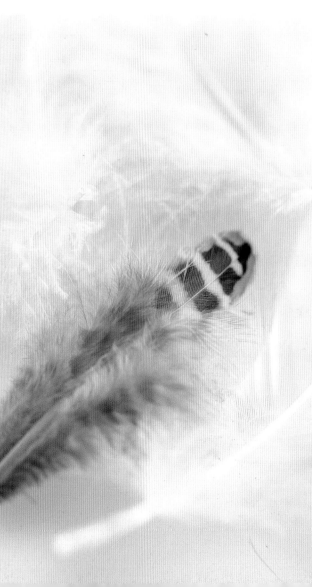

W eather permitting, choose a beautiful setting of your choice, perhaps a place that is of special importance to both of you. It can be woodland, a stone circle or someone's garden, or the ceremony can be performed indoors. Play some of your favourite music as a background to the ceremony. Each partner should invite an attendant and as many or as few guests as they like.

The bride and groom come to the sacred space, accompanied by their attendants. Together they face outwards to the east and the person who leads the ceremony invokes the spirits of the four quarters to bless the couple.

In the element of Air, I present [names] and ask for blessings upon them on this joyous day of their wedding, that they may gain clarity of vision towards one another, always communicate their thoughts and desires honestly and find lasting adventure in one other.

Gift ideas

■ Appropriate gifts or mementoes might be horse-shoes – old symbols of good luck – with coloured ribbons threaded through the holes to symbolize the elements (see right).

■ You can also give Welsh love spoons and other plants representing love in folklore. Chicory, for example, is a traditional aphrodisiac, and broom twigs tied with a ribbon have long been regarded as a symbol of good luck at a wedding.

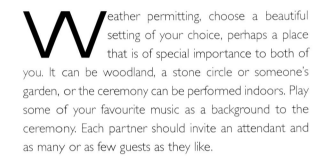

A cleansing chant for midsummer's day

I celebrate the noon of summer with mystic rites.

O Great Goddess and God,

All nature vibrates with your energies

And the earth is bathed with warmth and life.

Now is the time of forgetting past cares and banes;

Now is the time for purification.

O fiery Sun,

Burn away the Unuseful, the Hurtful, the Bane

In your omnipotent power

Purify Me! Purify Me! Purify Me!

Composed by Scott Cunningham

Welcoming
the harvest

The beginning of August should be a glorious time of year and it marks the gathering of the harvest. Yet this is, and always has been, an unpredictable affair, its success or failure dictated by the vagaries of the summer weather.

In days gone by a poor harvest automatically meant a winter of hardship, possibly starvation and death. Even today adverse conditions in the great grain belts of the United States or Russia can affect the climatic balance worldwide. As global warming proceeds relentlessly, increasing numbers of people are realizing that bringing back a proper reverence for the natural world is essential if the human race is to survive.

In Wicca and other pagan fellowships, the reaping of the harvest is linked with the Sabbat of Lammas or Lughnasadh, the rites of which extend far back into antiquity, to a time when the concept of the dying and rising God first took its place in our hearts. Pagan traditions maintain that the person who cuts the last of the field is the host into which the dying Corn Spirit flees as it is cut down by the Goddess wielding the sickle of death in her terrible aspect as the hag or crone. He thus becomes the human embodiment of the deity and must be 'sacrificed' symbolically in order to ensure the fertility of the crop in the following year.

The Corn Mother

■ The belief in a Corn Maiden and a Corn Mother has been very strong in Europe, equating with the Rice Mother in the Far East. The Greek fertility goddess, Demeter, who became Ceres for the Romans, was closely linked with both wheat and barley. All kinds of obscure and wonderful traditions have grown up associated with the idea that a goddess is actually represented in the 'corn' and is responsible for making it grow. When the cereal grasses wave in the summer wind it is said that the Corn Mother is

The ancient ritual of slaughter gave rise in English country lore to the figure of John Barleycorn, the ill-fated reaper of the last few stalks of the wheat. The final yard of the grain has possessed great spiritual significance for this reason. Often it was left standing until the Corn Mother, by now in her terrible aspect as the hag or crone of the dying year, had been beaten out and driven away by the reapers, after which it was cut by an old woman. According to some traditions, William Rufus was killed as a sacrifice victim at Lammas, since he died on 2 August, 1100.

There are conflicting explanations of the word Lammas. Either it is derived from the Celtic Lughnasadh or it may be a corruption of 'loaf mass', when the first corn was harvested and made into bread.

To perform a Lammas ceremony, first create your sacred circle with its altar, perhaps marking the four quarters with sheaves of grain. Sweep it ritually with twigs of birch or broom. The priestess or person who is to lead the ceremony should begin by invoking the guardians of the four quarters (see page 16). She calls upon the Goddess:

O Great and bountiful Mother of the Earth
You have bestowed your gift of fruitfulness upon us.
We give you our heartfelt thanks and we honour you

As we join together in celebration of the first fruits of
the harvest.

If there is also a priest present he should invoke the God:

O Great and generous Father
You have warmed and quickened the earth
You have given the gentle rain and wind that nurtured
the fruits of the season
We give you our heartfelt thanks and we honour you.

Everyone may now say these words in unison:

Let us be merry and glad on this day of harvest home.
We bid welcome to you, Great Mother and
Mighty Father,
And bid you stay to join our feast.

Each of the participants may now bring the Goddess and God a gift from the harvest and speak their own words of thanks as they place their offering on the altar. These gifts should include a loaf to symbolize the grain, some fruit, vegetables and milk, and finally someone should offer wine. The circle should be closed and those attending the ceremony should all join in a feast of the harvest bounty and wine.

---

passing through the field, but she is not always thought of as friendly and there have been old taboos against children going into the corn to pick flowers since the Corn Mother might catch them.

■ By the time the corn was ripe the Goddess had, as we saw above, definitely assumed the frightening aspect of the hag. It was believed that the harvest reapers effectively drove her into the last stand and the sheaf made from this carried special significance.

Sometimes it was weighed with stones at its centre to make it seem that it contained a body before it was carried home, but in other customs it was beaten with sticks to frighten out the Corn Mother. In slightly more elaborate rites it was modelled into the shape of a woman by the person who cut the last of the field, then dressed in a white sheet before being taken home. The village threshing floor, where the model was hung, was the place where the spirit of the corn was 'released' from the dying year.

Rites to perform
at the equinoxes

Unlike many pagan festivals, there is no equivalent of the Spring (or Vernal) and Autumn Equinoxes in the Christian calendar.

The Vernal Equinox or Eostre is marked on 20 and 21 March. After the winter the length of the night is at last reduced to that of the day. This is a wonderful time of year in the natural world, but we are experiencing global warming and so plants are blooming and animals becoming active earlier than previously. This year at the Equinox I discovered the first bluebells flowering in a wood behind my home, at least a month earlier than I had expected, interspersed with a riot of primroses, violets, celandines and wood anemones. It is said, incidentally, that picking the first violet you find in spring will bring you good luck for the rest of the year. Having become thoroughly euphoric about balmy spring days, however, the wind today is blowing from the north-east as I write this page. On 28 March it is bitterly cold and there is a hint of sleet in the air!

If we celebrate the Vernal Equinox, it is to mark the turning of the year rather than the arrival or departure of nature gods and goddesses and we should be out in the countryside at dawn. The English village witch Paddy Slade suggests that we should first open our sacred circle and then enact a symbolic struggle between Dark and Light. Two men in the group can perform a mock battle, at the culmination of which the combatant

The Autumn Equinox

■ The Autumn or Fall Equinox, celebrated between 20 and 21 September, marks the safe storage of the harvest. Our ceremony takes place at the end of the fruitful season and is the reverse of the celebrations at the Vernal Equinox. The turning point of the year between summer and winter is a fine time in nature. The Fall in New England and Vermont presents a glorious palette of russets and golds, the English autumn hedgerow is a riot of berries and seeds, European forests are filled with intoxicating smells of damp earth and fungi. Many years ago I discovered a glorious verse by Samuel Taylor Coleridge inscribed above the inglenook in an old Sussex pub and promptly learned it by heart.

I have desired and found the best of my desires in the autumn road,
The mellow winds that soothe the darkening shires
. . . and laughter
. . . and inn fires.

Autumn

The wheel turns on to Autumn time
The gods are strong and in their prime
We give our love and thanks anew
O God and Goddess, praise to you.
O power bring the balance in
As the Wheel retains its spin.

Paddy Slade

representing Dark is defeated and retires to the edge of the circle while the victorious Light stands at the centre. The Vernal Equinox is also known as the Festival of the Trees and this is also an appropriate time to invoke the Goddess and thank her for the new shoots of life that are erupting throughout the forests. We can open our sacred circle in a woodland and dance around it to greet both the Goddess of Greenery and the God of Light and Sun after asking their blessings. It may also be appropriate to ignite a small flame in a crucible to symbolize the growing sun – but *please* do not light naked fires in or near trees. After this amount of exercise, close the circle, go home and have a serious breakfast!

■ Our Autumn Equinox ceremony should also take place in the countryside by creating a sacred circle and bringing a guarded flame to symbolize the departing sun. We should invoke the Goddess and give thanks for the fruits of the summer season, now all around us, and each person should bring something from their own garden or window box to leave as an offering. Paddy Slade suggests that our circle dance might include the above chant.

A ceremony for
the midwinter solstice

In England the Ancient Druid Order is perhaps best known to the general public for its celebration of the longest day of the year at Stonehenge in Wiltshire, but Druids also mark the Winter Solstice and, for them, this is a more private occasion, a time for reflection.

It is the moment when the new Sun is born to the Great Mother, the turning point in the depth of winter when the world may look forward to the miracle of genesis in spring. Amergin Aryson, a member of the Ar nDraiocht Fein fellowship in the United States, has written a beautiful invocation for the Winter Solstice. It has been slightly modified to make it more suitable for a non-denominational celebration. If this ceremony is performed out of doors, as ideally it should be, you will need to find a tree stump or a large boulder to serve as an altar. You will also need a small number of items to be placed on the altar before the rite opens.

A branch of holly should be easy to find and the gift of gold does not have to be your best heirloom! How about some old man's beard or teasel fruits sprayed with inexpensive gold paint? A crucible to burn incense and a bowl or cauldron containing water with about an inch of aromatic oil and a floating wick are required. Remember to obtain permission from the landowner before you ignite any naked flame. Incense, hazelnuts and apples or some other offering of your personal choice complete the list.

Form a circle around the altar at midday. A man and a woman should lead the ceremony jointly and, if they wish, those who attend the ceremony may join in by repeating the last lines of each section in unison. The priest should speak these words first, standing and facing the winter sun in the south:

Beware the sun!

■ Please note one small but essential precaution if your celebration is held on a clear day. The rays of the winter sun, weak as they may seem, are immensely powerful. They can do permanent damage to your eyes, so do not stare straight at the sun, however briefly. Even the use of sunglasses or a smoked glass does not provide adequate protection.

Invocation for the winter solstice

Known are you by many names
by many peoples,
Yet always the same in your countenance.
O Shining, Radiant, Lovely One,
We behold your rebirth this day
In awe and reverence.

He holds aloft the offerings, first of gold then of holly,
after which he ignites the wick in the bowl of oil water
and finally burns the incense in the crucible.

We make offering to you of gold,
The shining tear of the sun.
We make offering to you of the sacred holly,
The ever green and ever growing.
We make offering to you of oil and incense,
So your flame may grow in
strength and brilliance.
We make the offering to the Sacred Fire.
O beloved, newborn son of the
Great Mother,
Accept our worship and our praise,
And grant us your blessings.
Grow strong, O newborn Sun.

The woman who is to act as the priestess now invokes
the Goddess.

She who is the Great Mother,
She who is, this day, the veiled crone of
Stark Winter
Known are you by many names
by many peoples,
Yet always the same in your countenance.
O shadowy, Hidden and Haggard one,
We behold your great mystery this day,
In awe and reverence.

She holds aloft the hazelnuts, followed by the apples,
and then she, too, burns incense in the crucible.

We make offering to you of hazelnuts,
The kernel of knowledge from
your sacred tree.
We make offering to you of apples,
The fruit of the Blessed Isle of Death
and Rebirth.
We make the offering to the Sacred Fire.
O Great, Mysterious, Veiled One,
Accept our worship and our praise.
Grant us your blessings.

The Yule log:
light in the darkness

One of the special and time-honoured events associated with the Winter Solstice is the bringing in and lighting of the Yule log.

This act amounts to a symbolic placing of trust, on the darkest night of the year, in the Dark Lord of Winter. It underlines our belief that the wheel of nature will turn and that spring will come again. It also embodies the purifying power of fire, which immolates the life of the old year and provides nourishing ashes for the new. Nobody knows for certain where the tradition originated. It may have come first from the ancient civilizations of Mesopotamia, where the idea of the sacred tree embodying either the Mother Goddess or the dying and rising god arose and where stylized trees were first decorated. But the Norsemen are also strong claimants. It is suggested that they revered the Yule log as a symbol of the world tree, the sacred ash known as Yggdrasil, and that they began the practice of lighting a Yule log which was kept burning through the festivities. Its flames celebrated the return of the sun to their dark northern winter world. The origin of the association between mistletoe and Yule also comes from Norse tradition, since it was the weapon used in midwinter inadvertently to slay Balder, the favourite son of the Father God, Othin.

How do I make a Yule log?

■ According to tradition the log should not be bought but should be collected either from one's own or someone else's land. Today, unfortunately, hauling a length of oak or ash out of woodland that does not belong to you can bring less than favourable repercussions, so compromise may be necessary! Try, if possible, to compensate the owner with something other than money – perhaps a bottle of wine. The log must be decorated with evergreen material before lighting. Holly and ivy are obvious choices, but you can also use bits of fir bough and perhaps some coloured ribbons.

■ Once decorated, the log is laid in the hearth (assuming you have one) ready for lighting. If you are preparing a Yule log for the first time, use whatever kindling is at your disposal, but ideally it should be ignited using kindling from the remains of last year's log. These should have been kept for 12 months in a convenient box in a dry place.

> In the cold depths of winter, when the natural world seems to have died, the igniting of a yule log symbolized the light and warmth of summer sun that we ask the gods to bring back to us.

Seasonal traditions from around the world

■ Midwinter

In the more hilly part of the eastern Netherlands they used to set light to a cartwheel and send it rolling down a slope accompanied by the blowing of horns, its flaming shape symbolizing the return of the sun.

■ Midsummer

Water is a powerful symbol of life, and we can perform a simple ritual of magical renewal by pouring water over one another on midsummer day as they do in parts of Russia. A similar custom in Sweden is to bathe in a river, so invoking the Goddess to bring life-giving rain. It may not be safe to copy this but there is no reason why we cannot splash ourselves with water taken from a clean stream.

According to some traditions the oldest male member of the family should perform the lighting ceremony, and a small prayer must be said asking the God for protection for family and friends and for all living things in nature through the dark and unpredictable days ahead.

■ A nice idea, again drawn from tradition, is to sprinkle the log with grain from the harvest and with a little cider – these constitute a small gift of thanks, a sacrifice to the God of winter. Once the log is lit it should be burnt for a specific length of time. This, however, will depend on the size of your hearth which, in turn, will determine the size of the log! The minimum time should be twelve hours, but in some traditions the log is kept smouldering for the whole twelve days of Christmas. In any event it is important that the wood is not completely burnt away. It must be extinguished while there is still a portion left, to keep and use as the kindling for next year's Yule log.

CHAPTER 5

Celebrating
marriage and other relationships

Marriage must surely represent

the most popular of ceremonies

involving rites of passage, yet

surprisingly little has been

preserved about wedding rituals

of our pagan past. How were

they conducted? What order of

words was used? What was

their legal binding?

Alternative ways
to celebrate marriage

Little has been preserved about marriage rituals. A possible reason is that weddings were so commonplace and their format so widely known that no one bothered to pass on the details of the actual ritual, either by word of mouth or, later, by writing it down.

Like most alternative rituals, the weddings that take place today, including those of Wicca and other variations on the theme of wedlock, are not authentic copies of ancient rituals. They are reconstructions of the ways in which we believe, for the most part romantically rather than from archaeological or historical findings, that our ancestors may have celebrated such occasions.

Wicca marriage is more commonly known as hand-fasting and it includes the taking of vows, the exchanging of rings and a celebratory feast. The ceremony is generally led by the high priestess or priest of a coven and guests either wear white or attend sky-clad.

What kind of commitment should I make?

The Christian marriage ceremony is still based largely on social values and economic conditions that date back, in part, to the medieval period when there were no effective contraceptives and no social welfare systems. In times gone by it was largely because of these considerations that people were obliged to enter wedlock for life. These days many people getting married in alternative ceremonies are more reluctant to make the Christian promise 'until death us do part', accepting that it is increasingly unrealistic as an initial level of undertaking. They prefer to agree to remain in partnership for as long as love lasts, after which each is permitted to leave the relationship and go their separate ways. The emphasis must remain, however, on mutual promises and an honourable partnership wherein, if one or other party feels unable to keep the promises they made at their wedding, they must take no less honourable steps to end the partnership. Not everyone would agree with such liberalization and some will still wish to make a lifelong declaration. For further inspiration see page 98.

Just as we need to have alternative ceremonies to make a partnership official, so too we must include rituals to formalize a parting because not all marriages, by whatever name or creed, will last a lifetime. There is no legal obligation to end them through the courts unless they have been instigated in a church or registry office with state involvement, in which case they must, of course, be terminated according to the law of the land.

An alternative marriage rite

The pagan Nigel Pearson has contributed a marriage ceremony based on the one which he wrote for the gay handfasting with his partner, Anthony Moorhouse. This modified form is, however, also appropriate for a heterosexual ceremony.

The priest and couple enter the sacred sircle and stand in silent contemplation for a moment before each places lighted candles on the altar. The priest now lights a candle to the north of the circle, saying:

I invoke the Spirits of the North, of Life and Death,
of Earth and Strength to be with us and witness
this rite of Marriage.

He moves to light candles to the east, then south and west with the following words:

I invoke the spirits of the East, of birth and creation,
of air and mind to be with us and witness
this rite of Marriage.
I invoke the spirits of the South, of growth and energy,
of fire and passion to be with us and witness
this rite of Marriage.
I invoke the spirits of the West, of knowledge and
wisdom, of water and love to be with us and witness
this rite of Marriage.

The Priest returns to the altar and blesses the salt and water.

I bless this salt, the oldest rock and the oldest
cleanser, to hold the sacred spirit of this rite.
I bless this water, the sustainer of life and the ripple
of creation, to hold the sacred spirit of this rite.

He mixes salt and water together and sprinkles the mixture round the edge of the circle, beginning at the north, before sprinkling the couple at the altar. Incense is also used to purify the circle.

The Goddess is now invoked to join the Marriage Rite:

O boundless Goddess of infinite light, triple-aspected
One of the sacred land and starry heavens,
everlasting queen and mother of both gods and
mankind, extend thy protection and blessing upon this
Rite of Marriage!
We bear witness to thy sacred Law of Life in the
bodies of these two who will be joined.
Pour forth thy gracious spirit upon their union
and imbue their lives together with thy
changeless essence.
Bless them O infinite Goddess of Heaven and Earth
with awareness of thee and of themselves,
in joy and love for the length of their days.
Blessed be O Supreme Goddess, in all thy many
names and manifold attributes.

The God is invoked likewise:

O Mighty God of boundless strength, energy of the
solar orb and power of the forests,
great Father and protector of all Earth's folk,
bring joy and compassion to this Rite of Marriage.
Great Horned One, the power of life is in thy laugh
and vitality springs from thy very presence;
be here now therefore and bring thy divine
inebriation to the joining of these two, that they may
share in the infinite pleasure of life continuing.
Make them aware of thee and of the oneness
of all in union.

Blessed be O mighty God, in all thy many names and manifold attributes.

Leading the couple to each quarter, the priest says:

Spirits of the North, bring to this union the qualities of the wolf, the essence of steadfastness.
Spirits of the East, bring to this union the qualities of the hawk, the essence of freedom.
Spirits of the South, bring to this union the qualities of the dragon, the essence of passion.
Spirits of the West, bring to this union the qualities of the salmon, the essence of wisdom.

The Couple then return to the altar and make a pledge to each other, before witnesses and using their own words. They then recite a blessing to each other:

You are the star of each night,
You are the brightness of every morning,
You are the story of each guest,
You are the report of every land.
No evil shall befall you.
On hill nor bank, in field or valley,
on mountain or in glen.
Neither above nor below,
Neither in sea nor on shore,
In skies above nor in depths.
You are the kernel of my heart,
You are the face of my sun.
You are the harp of my music,
You are the crown of my company.

In the Joining the priest asks each partner to repeat:

By seed and root, by bud and stem, by leaf and flower and fruit, by life and love, in the names of the God and Goddess, I, (name), take thee, (name), to my hand, my heart and my spirit, at the setting of the sun and the rising of the stars. Nor shall death part us; for in the fullness of time we shall be born again at

the same time and in the same place as each other; and we shall meet and know and remember and love again.

He then says:

These two people have pledged themselves to each other.
Now as a symbol before all beings, gods and men, that they be really joined,
do I hold forth the reality of their Joining.

He offers the wand to the couple, threaded with the rings, and each partner places a ring on the other's finger, uttering their own words before the priest ties their hands together with a red ribbon. He places his hands over theirs, saying:

What was two, now becomes one.

Still joined by the ribbon and witnessed by the priest, the couple embrace and, hands now freed, sign a scroll before being led round the Circle, beginning at the north.

May the blessings of the ancestors and of the earth be upon you.
May the blessings of birth and of the air be upon you.
May the blessings of fertility and of the fire be upon you.
May the blessings of fulfilment and of the water be upon you.

The priest delivers his final blessing:

Power of raven be yours; power of eagle be yours.
Power of Storm be yours; power of moon be yours; power of sun.
Power of sea be yours; power of land be yours; power of heaven.
Each day be joy to you; no day be sad to you; Honour and tenderness.

The wine and cakes are blessed:

I call a blessing on this wine, that all who partake of
it may be refreshed in mind, body and soul.
In the names of the God and Goddess, so be it!
I call a blessing on these cakes, that all who partake
of them may be refreshed in mind, body and soul.
In the names of the God and Goddess, so be it!

The guests repeat, *So be it*, as appropriate.

The priest now takes a sip of wine and passes it to the
couple to drink, then takes cake and passes it likewise.

With the wine he says: *May you never thirst.*
With the cake he says: *May you never hunger.*
The priest then scatters a cake and pours some wine on
the ground as an offering to the deities.

The spirits of the quarters are now thanked and dis-
missed. At each quarter the candle is extinguished with
the words Hail and farewell, repeated by the guests.

Spirits of the North, of earth and strength,
we thank thee for thine attendance and aid at this
Rite of Marriage.
Spirits of the East, of air and mind,
we thank thee for thine attendance and aid at this
Rite of Marriage.
Spirits of the South, of fire and passion,
we thank thee for thine attendance and aid at this
Rite of Marriage.
Spirits of the West, of Water and Love,
we thank thee for thine attendance and aid at this
Rite of Marriage.

The priest goes widdershins around the circle, sweeping
it away with the broom. On completion he lays the
broomstick down on the ground and steps aside. The
couple join hands and jump over the broomstick to seal
their union, then pass the cakes and wine to the guests.

A simple
wedding ceremony

The high priestess Caroline Wise has provided the basis for this version of a non-denominational marriage that we can all use and adapt as we wish.

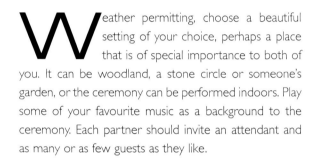

Weather permitting, choose a beautiful setting of your choice, perhaps a place that is of special importance to both of you. It can be woodland, a stone circle or someone's garden, or the ceremony can be performed indoors. Play some of your favourite music as a background to the ceremony. Each partner should invite an attendant and as many or as few guests as they like.

The bride and groom come to the sacred space, accompanied by their attendants. Together they face outwards to the east and the person who leads the ceremony invokes the spirits of the four quarters to bless the couple.

In the element of Air, I present [names] and ask for blessings upon them on this joyous day of their wedding, that they may gain clarity of vision towards one another, always communicate their thoughts and desires honestly and find lasting adventure in one other.

Gift ideas

■ Appropriate gifts or mementoes might be horse-shoes – old symbols of good luck – with coloured ribbons threaded through the holes to symbolize the elements (see right).

■ You can also give Welsh love spoons and other plants representing love in folklore. Chicory, for example, is a traditional aphrodisiac, and broom twigs tied with a ribbon have long been regarded as a symbol of good luck at a wedding.

The attendants hand the couple each a gift symbolizing the air – perhaps a nice feather – and then they turn to the north.

In the element of Earth, I present [names] and ask the blessings of a stable home, financial security, good health and patience with one another.

The gift here might be a lovely pebble or stone, particularly one with a hole in it, known as a 'hagstone', to protect them from evil. The couple turns to the south and the leader of the ceremony invokes again.

In the element of fire, I present [names] that their passions may burn long, that they may be creative towards one another and sustain the will to keep their bond of marriage loyal and true.

The gift handed to each partner here may be a candle or a recording of some appropriately passionate music. Finally the couple turn to the west.

In the element of water, I present [names]. May their love last, may their dreams be fulfilled and may good things flow to them.

Some appropriate gifts associated with water might be a lovely seashell, a goblet or a glass bowl with pebbles. These gifts can cost nothing or very little, in fact only as much as the guest wishes to spend. The important thing is that they will be kept in a special place along with photos of the occasion, cards and messages from well-wishers.

At the end of the blessing ceremony the couple should toast each other with champagne, arms entwined as the guests shower them with rose petals. The rose is a flower of love and is sacred to Aphrodite. You will no doubt want to follow the ceremony with a little more drink and some food!

Elemental gifts

■ All kinds of fertility symbols have been used at one time or another in wedding ceremonies but one of the easiest to make is a little sheaf of corn tied with a ribbon.

■ For traditional weddings in Austria they make iced gingerbreads in the shape of hearts, but any crescent-shaped cakes and biscuits, symbols of the Goddess, can be offered.

coloured ribbons: ■ yellow for air ■ orange for fire ■ green for earth ■ blue for water ■ red for love

■ The presents we give to symbolize the elements are very significant. They are not merely representations of the material plane but are found on the etherial plane and the astral plane. They are the elementals and the elemental rulers.

The sacred
marriage in Wicca

In Wicca the Marriage, otherwise known as the Great Rite, is at the core of the third degree of initiation for a witch, the highest level for those who have already become members of the movement and who wish to form their own covens as high priests and high priestesses.

Its symbol is an upward-pointing pentagram, representing life, crowned with a small triangle. The essence of the Sacred Marriage is that the *animus* (male spirituality) or *anima* (female spirituality) of the initiate becomes as one with his or her opposite. It is performed either symbolically or as an authentic sexual coupling of priest and priestess and the sacred circle is restricted to third degree initiates.

The Sacred Marriage is not, as some sensationalist authors would have it, an excuse for a sex orgy, but relies on the belief that nature depends on the interplay of opposite forces. As Dorien Valiente once said, 'if all witches wanted was sex orgies they would have not had to invent a witch cult in order to indulge in them'.

The Great Rite is a sacred and exclusive ceremony and I have, therefore, provided only outline details here, following a description by Vivianne Crowley. At the outset the God and Goddess are invoked into those who will lead the ceremony, the high priest and priestess of the coven, and the woman of the partnership takes the initiation first. She is led to the altar and the initiator, representing the God in his aspect as Lord of Darkness, moves to the west, the quarter of death, before walking anti-clockwise, or widdershins, back to the initiate to take her through a symbolic death before rebirth. The process is repeated, with variations, for the male initiate who is directed by the Goddess in her aspect as the hag of old age. If he accepts her she walks to the east, discards her haggish guise and reveals herself as the youthful goddess of life.

At this juncture a bell is rung six times and the ceremonial sword and broomstick are laid crosswise on the ground at the north-east of the circle, whereupon

the male initiate, in a black cloak, stands behind them and is challenged by the high priestess. If he responds correctly he is admitted to the Sacred Marriage rite.

In a token Sacred Marriage the female initiate now lies on the ground, spreadeagled, with her head to the north, the *athame* by her right hand and a chalice of wine by her left. The high priest first stands between her thighs holding a spear, then he kneels, kisses her and invokes the goddess into her through symbolic words and gestures. Finally he draws her into a kneeling position and offers her the chalice. She is now the temple of the Goddess, the womb of the earth.

In a full act of the Sacred Marriage, the initiated priestess now unites with the priest, who is, in effect, at the half-way stage of his initiation. She lies on the ground, as

before, and much of the same procedure is repeated but this time the initiate priest stands between her thighs. The high priest and priestess now open the circle and everyone except the initiates retire to a discreet distance where they remain until the act of union is completed. It is this act of sexual coupling that lies at the heart of belief in the divinities of nature. Out of death has come the miracle of regenesis, from the ashes of the old have arisen the saplings of the new life. The life-giving semen of the god penetrates and fertilizes the womb of the earth, just as the rain from the skies brings germination to a seemingly barren soil.

The priestess, still acting as the embodiment of the Goddess, offers the priest the chalice and the other members of the coven are summoned back to the circle. The ceremony is followed by a feast of celebration.

A folk marriage
from India

If you like the idea of an alternative wedding from an Eastern tradition, the following marriage ceremony from India may appeal. Marriage in India has been formalized within the law but it still follows a pattern based on ancient rites.

In India an astrologer will be called upon before the marriage. He will determine the most auspicious date and time, known as the *muhurta*, to solemnize the ritual. India has long been a more male-dominated society than we have grown used to in the West and the ceremony can be freely varied to give the bride a stronger participation in the ritual.

What do we do?

When everyone is assembled the groom makes a small sacrifice on the altar with his right hand while the bride holds his left. The sacrifice can be an object entirely symbolic of the love between the bride and groom, or some small personal possession. It will not be necessary to slay a chicken. The bridegroom then faces west, the bride east while he says:

I take thy hand in mine for happy fortune.

He then takes her thumb if he wishes for sons, the other fingers for daughters and the whole hand for boys and girls. The bride may choose to reiterate these words.

The bridegroom leads his bride three times around the altar clockwise saying,

I am this, you are she; I am heaven, you are earth. Let us marry each other, raise sons and daughters, be kind to each other, friendly, with well-meaning mind may we live a hundred years.

The stone possesses an important symbolic function. Each time the bride must step on the grinding-stone (see page 103) while the groom says:

Be firm as this stone, overcome adversity.

Again, the roles may be reversed according to preference.

The person who is officiating may now sprinkle rose petals over the hands of the couple three times. The groom next unties the hair-band or ribbon of his partner, saying:

I deliver you from the bonds of Varuna (a major god in India).

If the groom is also wearing a band, his bride may repeat these actions and words. The man now asks his bride to take seven steps to the north as he says:

May you take a step for power, a step from strength, one for wealth, one for fortune, one for children, one for good times. With the seventh step may we be each other's friend, be faithful one to another and live long.

The person who officiates takes the jug, brings the heads of the couple together and sprinkles them with the water. They may then exchange rings, after which the ceremony is complete, and a celebratory feast should follow.

What is needed?

■ The marriage rite, *vivaha samskara*, is performed around an altar, which can be any suitable surface from a living-room table to a weathered slab of granite. The only essential requirement is that a 'fire' can be placed on it in a form as simple as a lighted candle or a crucible of incense. If out in the country-side, please do not accidentally ignite large tracts of forest or the wedding may take on some unusual aspects! To the west of the fire must be placed a grinding-stone (use your imagination if you normally buy your flour from a supermarket) and to the north-east a jug containing water. Dress is entirely optional but the bride, and if so desired the groom, should wear some form of hair-band or ribbon. Someone must also be chosen to officiate, perhaps a close friend.

A European
wedding ceremony

We need to remember that at some time or other many of the ceremonies now regarded as 'alternative' have been worked into, or formed a basis for, that which is termed orthodox, *a word which simply means 'the correct path'.*

Much of the pagan ritual of Europe found its way into Christianity, Judaism borrowed heavily from the older faiths of the ancient Near East, and modern Hinduism arose out of a much older folk culture. For many centuries, however, the monolithic religions jealously guarded their 'right to rule' by discouraging any form of dissent. The ritual of marriage has been a good example, because it is not only in India that many of the familiar wedding traditions are based on ancient pagan rites.

The choice of ritual in a pagan wedding is, of course, yours and mine to do as we will. Here is a suggestion, however, based on the recent marriage of a pagan, Stormerne Hunt-Anschutz, which took place in a log cabin 8,000 feet up in the Rocky Mountains of North America.

In the cabin, an altar was prepared that included two small statues of deities from Viking tradition – Var, the ninth among a sorority of goddesses linked with Othin and known as the Asynuir, and Bragi, the Norse god of poetry and oration. The wedding rings were also placed on the altar in company with the hammer of Thor, an important symbol of fertility, an oath ring and a horn for drinking mead. The rings had been crafted and engraved with runic inscriptions which represented not only the names of the couple but also the archaic words for 'dear' and 'beloved'. Runes are the symbols and sounds, arranged in sets of eight to form an alphabet, that were used by the Germanic and Scandinavian peoples, often for magical purposes, until the end of the Viking era.

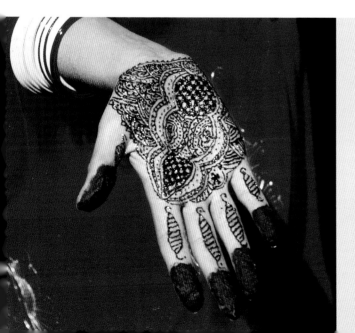

Painting the hands

■ Anything which can make a bride-to-be feel pampered and important on her wedding day is to be welcomed. In the West we have grown used to all kinds of small home-grown rituals associated with Christian marriage preparations, but there are others well worth considering from different parts of the world.

Stormerne and his bride-to-be started their ritual by praising one another publicly and explaining why they wanted each other as husband and wife. Grasping the oathring, they declared the vows that they had prepared to one another and then took up Thor's hammer, each blessing a wedding ring and placing it on the other's finger while saying, 'Consecrate us together by the hand of Var.' The horn, first sanctified with the hammer, was filled with mead and used to toast the newly forged bond, while the hammer was placed in the bride's lap.

To conform to legal requirements, Stormerne and his bride then signed marriage documents in the presence of witnesses. Finally the horn, refilled with mead at regular intervals, was passed around the guests for ritual toastings not only to the couple but also to Othin, Thor and Freya, the Vanir goddess of love, marriage and prosperity. Following another old tradition, Stormerne formally presented the keys of the house to his new wife and, on the morning after the wedding, they exchanged gifts.

Symbols of marriage

■ rings ■ knots

The ring and the knot have long been associated with weddings. The knot symbolizes firm attachment and so, in different parts of the world, a bridegroom is often decked with pieces of knotted net on tight knotted girdles. In Russia, there has been a tradition of using skeins of wool that are wrapped around the arms and legs.

■ A pretty ceremony involving the women friends and relatives of a girl before she gets married also comes from Indian tradition. The hands are painted with special patterns using henna dye. Until recently it was difficult to obtain the materials or the details of how to craft the patterns, but kits for hand painting are now available from various occult outlets. For more information see page 140.

A ritual
of separation

Even if a partnership is ended through an alternative rite, it is sensible that it should be witnessed in writing and certified by an official notary.

It is important, as with any serious and inevitably consequential decision, that such an act should not be taken lightly and, if it is agreed upon, the parting should be overseen by a priest or priestess and by at least two independent witnesses. The person who officiates should also be prepared to serve, prior to the parting, as an arbitrator on such matters as division of property and the provision of financial and material support for any children of the partnership.

What kind of ceremony?

Nothing need be elaborate, but the room or open space where the parting is to take place should be prepared in the manner described earlier in this book in order to make its circle sacred for the purpose. An altar will be needed either at the centre or towards the western edge of the circle, which, in the northern hemisphere, is the direction of the setting sun. In a Wicca handparting the altar will be equipped with candles, an incense burner and a ceremonial dagger or *athame*.

At the opening of the ceremony the candles and incense are lit and the priest or priestess stands before the assembled participants to consecrate the circle. If so desired, the wrists of the parting couple may be loosely tied to symbolize the fact that they are still joined.

The priest or priestess may begin with the words:

In the presence of the old and shining ones, we are met, solemnly, in this sacred place, to sever the cord which has bound [name] and [name] as one. Come forward now and stand in the presence of the god and goddess and the spirits of nature.

The words of the ceremony can be varied, but the priest or priestess must ask of the couple, for the final time and before witnesses, if they wish to part. Each must be challenged by name and each must answer clearly, yes or no. If one or other does not agree to the parting then matters must be postponed until further counselling has taken place. Ultimately, though, if one partner continues to insist then the parting must proceed with or without the compliance of the other.

In pagan ceremonies, a photograph or a symbolic model of the couple may be placed on the altar at the start of the ceremony. This is then handed to them so that they may jointly tear it up or break it apart in some other manner. The pieces are taken by the person officiating, who will ignite them in the crucible or burn them in the flame of one of the candles.

A ceremony for separation

Wicca ceremonies of handfasting, which take place in the presence of the Goddess and God, will include an invocation along these lines:

We beseech you, O blessed ones, to bring your healing comfort to soften the distress and pain of those who have come before us this day to part. As they travel their separate paths towards the future, let not bitterness and antagonism towards the past cloud their hearts but may they part in a spirit of concern for each other, remembrance of the life which they have shared, and a love for each other as fellow human beings.

The priest or priestess will now take up the *athame* and sever the cord binding the wrists, instructing the two people that they are now free to go their separate ways. No apportionment of blame is attached to the rite of handfasting. The sacred circle is finally closed.

CHAPTER 6

Performing alternative ceremonies

One of the attractions of alternative ceremonies is that we are free to perform them in whichever way we see fit. The choices of how and where are ours so long as we keep within the laws of the country in which we live.

The significance
of propitiation and prayer

In many traditions, from Native American to Chinese Taoist, worshippers still practice sacred ceremonies directed towards the spirits of their ancestors. They are designed specifically to ask mercy towards the living and to provide a comfort for the dead.

When I think of propitiation to the spirit world, asking atonement for our failings, I am often reminded of a lovely poem by Matthew Arnold called 'Balder Dead'. Balder, the ill-fated child of the Norse god Othin, the dying and rising son, was killed by an innocent sprig of mistletoe turned magically into a lethal dart. Yet he was also restored to a world cleansed and renewed because the gods heard the weeping of humanity.

In all the forests, and the soft-strewn snow
Under the trees is dibbled thick with holes
And from the boughs the snow loads shuffle down;
And, in fields sloping to the south, dark plots
Of grass peep out amid surrounding snow,
And widen, and the peasant's heart is glad –
So through the world was heard a dripping noise
Of all things weeping to bring Balder back,
And there fell joy upon the Gods to hear.

Those of us who possess a belief in the spirit world generally accept that we should show the divine powers not only our thanks and joy, but also our grief and remorse when appropriate. In Arnold's poem the world weeps on behalf of the God whose life has been cruelly extinguished through the dark days of winter. The deities hear our anguished prayers and respond joyously with the first glimpse of spring thaw.

In the Christian faith, prayer and the act of propitiation have largely become mechanical. The most extreme

form is seen in Roman Catholicism, where the rosary prayers have turned into little more than a *mantra*. The 150 beads of the rosary were once used as an aid to reciting the Psalter. This lengthy practice was eventually replaced, of considerable advantage to those who needed salvation but could not read or spare the time, by chanting the same number of Hail Marys.

Drawing strength from nature

We probably do not realize how many small impulses we follow in our daily lives that amount to acts of invocation and propitiation towards the spirit world. Our ancestry provides our family tree, and we touch wood for luck without realizing the implication that we are asking for the spiritual strength of a sacred tree, the World Ash or Yggdrasil. Sacred trees have been largely purged from our memories yet in the ancient world they symbolized the constant and powerful presence of the great Mother Goddess.

We dance around the maypole to celebrate the spring but, in seeming contradiction, we fear to bring the blossoms of the may tree into our homes. These are the vestiges of rites and taboos that were well understood by people in past centuries. We place small straw figures known as corn dollies in our houses yet we realize

little of their purpose to appease the Corn Mother by making sacred replicas of her Corn Baby. Even the Christian establishment is not immune to such 'irrational behaviour'. The Pope kisses the earth beneath his feet – hard to explain in Christian terms, yet seemingly plainly symbolic of our need for unity and harmony with the natural world.

The ceremonies, involving prayers and hymns of repentance, are believed to free the dead from suffering in the underworld and to deliver humanity from distress and catastrophe. In this chapter we will be looking at various ways in which we may invoke the spirit guardians – to gain their blessing, calm their anger, or act as a channel for their immense potential sources of energy.

Inspirational places in which to pray

- on top of a mountain
- beside a beautiful lake or river
- in your home

Rituals of
purification

Many cultures recognize a strong need for the leaders and participants in sacred ceremonies to cleanse themselves spiritually before taking part in rituals.

In the great Norse sagas it was believed that the world would end in a tremendous apocalypse known as Ragnarok, during which the earth would be cleansed, first by an all-consuming fire and then by the waters of a great flood. For us, in our alternative ceremonies, the strongest agents of purification are also fire and water. We can base our purification rites, symbolically, on these two elements by placing a crucible with a flame upon our altar and, before it, a cauldron of water. We then ask our spirit guardians, humbly, that the fire and the water purify our inner beings just as they scour away the impurities of our material world.

In the East, followers of Taoism, which translates as 'The Way', consider that rituals of purification are essential to ensure that a person is in a proper state of mind and body when they encounter the spiritual powers. Cleansing rituals are therefore conducted before any sacred ceremony is performed. In China they are based on traditions that extend back into very ancient times when the tribal rulers, who were also the shamans or priests, celebrated the spring planting and the autumn harvest. They prepared themselves to invoke the spiritual powers of sky and earth in carefully laid-down rites. Later these old traditions became incorporated into 'The Way' and became known as the rules of *chai*.

The importance of Zen

■ Zen, derived from Buddhism and probably introduced first into China in about 527CE is another spiritual discipline practised in the East in which purification features strongly as a preliminary to ritual, and it is coupled with a specific need for repentance. Zen Buddhists frequently confess their sins, though in private rather than through the interaction with a priest in a confessional that is

Since early times the two most important elements of purification have included fire and water – nature's own way of cleansing.

Westerners tend to imagine that *chai* is all about practising vegetarianism to rid the body of impurities but, in reality, the discipline extends a lot further than abstinence from eating meat. In Taoism ceremonies of purification can begin as much as three days before a major festival, and they involve not only the cleansing of the body but also the purification of the mind so that one's spiritual being is able to merge with 'The Way'. These ceremonies are not intended to be ascetic in the manner that strict Hindu or Buddhist devotees will deprive themselves of bodily comfort. Someone who is to conduct a festival rite as a lay person need only observe the disciplines during the day of the ritual or, at most, from the previous evening.

Bodily purification includes a strict dietary regime of abstinence from meat and dairy products but also requires a degree of fasting (see page 121). The person is required to give up all sexual activity during this period of preparation and to practise 'feeding on the breath of Tao'. He or she will engage in taking deep breaths of the misty air of early morning and in metaphysically 'swallowing' the celestial light of sun, moon and stars.

The person who is to lead a ceremonial rite will also prepare themselves mentally. All physical activity is reduced to a minimum – they withdraw from the hustle and bustle of life and enter into quiet seclusion to rid the mind of material issues.

more familiar to us in the West. A follower of Zen will pray by admitting fault and asking for protection from the Buddha while renewing his or her resolve to improve. Ridding oneself of spiritual impurity is considered essential before conducting a Zen sacred celebration, and the open expression of repentance through the shedding tears is often needed.

The act of purification

■ The act of purification can be conducted first by a symbolic physical cleaning using a broom, then with water that has been purified by the addition of salt.

■ Pure spring water is generally used by witches with a simple prayer of exorcism to cast out the impurities.

Using herbs
for rituals

In pagan traditions, invocation of the spirit powers often requires the use of herbs that possess magical properties. Many such plants can be found in the countryside, but there is also much to be said for growing your own in the kind of old-fashioned herb garden that, in bygone times, every wise woman possessed.

She would know by heart the plants from which to concoct magical sachets, incenses, aromatic oils and charms as well as those for use in simples and other remedies.

The range of magical and healing plants is considerable, so you have plenty of choice, but if you decide to grow your own you will be limited by the size of your garden, the soil type and the climate. Work out in advance what will grow well in your neck of the woods. The four herbs included below, however, which are all easy to grow, will give you a good staple 'rump', based on widespread country traditions.

Vervain was believed by the ancient Persians to possess aphrodisiac properties and in Germany a wreath of vervain was traditionally presented to the newly married bride. It has also been a guard against evil and has long been associated with witches' salves and ointments. At midsummer people wore vervain and mugwort garlands that were then tossed into a bonfire with the words, 'May all my ill-luck depart and be burnt with these.'

Mugwort has also been associated with midsummer, and its juice has been considered beneficial in clairvoyance as well as being a powerful protection against evil. The silvery texture of the under-surface of the leaves links it with the Moon Goddess and she is sometimes drawn with a spray of mugwort in her hand. A sprig of mugwort in the shoes before a journey is said to offset fatigue.

Rosemary was considered by the old herbalists to possess remedial properties in its aromatic oil. The Romans used it in their funeral rites because the lasting green of the leaves makes it a natural symbol of immortality and, in the north of England, sprays of rosemary are still sometimes thrown on to a coffin before the grave is filled.

Yarrow has long been valued for its healing properties and is a respected herb in the arts of divination and witchcraft, though it is generally accepted that it must be cut on the night of the full moon to be effective. *The Folk Lore Record* of 1878 includes this quaint rhyme recited by young girls in love, based on the contradictory fact that yarrow has been used both to encourage and to staunch nosebleeds!

Green 'arrow, green 'arrow, you wears a white bow;
If my love love me, my nose will bleed now;
If my love dont love me, it 'ont bleed a drop;
If my love do love me, 'twill bleed every drop.

Other herbs with powerful magical properties are considered valuable in more specific rituals. Those associated with love include lavender, lemon balm, lovage, old-fashioned roses, and violets. Plants with magical healing powers include carnation, garlic, rue, sage and wood sorrel.

Harvesting and drying herbs:

■ Herbs should be collected sparingly early in the season, followed by several major harvests when they are in full bloom, particularly in July and September. Start picking early in the day, after the dew has evaporated but before the sun has dissipated the essential oils. These are most concentrated when the flower buds are just about to open. Handle the material as little as possible. Herbs are best dried by hanging them in bunches in a dry but shady place in the house with a maximum circulation of air. Make

Eight herbs you can dry

■ rosemary ■ vervain ■ rue
■ chicory ■ mugwort ■ sage
■ wood sorrel ■ lavender

sure they are labelled, because you may not be able to identify them when dried! Store in airtight containers.

Herbs and plants
for different occasions

Although many herbs are understood to possess powerful magical properties, we have largely lost our understanding of these powers. In the great herbals, the 'medicine chests' of yesteryear, these qualities contributed, at least in part, to the selection process.

Herbs and other plants were considered to be governed by astral influences and this was often reflected in their therapeutic properties. A herb such as rosemary, ruled by the sun and of a warm disposition, was considered appropriate in the treatment of illnesses such the common cold which made the patient feel shivery. The therapeutic use of herbs is a matter that needs to be treated with great caution and it is not within the scope of this book. The magical associations of certain herbs are, however, valuable for us to know.

The American pagan and herbalist Autumn Crystal Greywing has contributed much of the information in the following lists of suitable herbs for different occasions, and I have amplified it from Culpeper's *British Herbal*. In some cases you will need to keep a supply of the dried herbs because when you need them they may be 'out-of-season' and not necessarily available fresh.

Herbs for Sabbats

SAMHAIN
Rosemary, mullein, pumpkin, apple, wormwood, mugwort, nettle, garlic and also any other herbs that have a magical association with divination and/or psychic powers. Hazel must be among the best known of these, but don't forget clover and yarrow. The famous oracle of Delphi gained her clairvoyant powers by chewing on the leaves of bay.

WINTER SOLSTICE (YULE)
Balsam, bay, holly, mistletoe, cinnamon, wintergreen, apple, cedar and also any evergreen, and any plant with the planetary association of the sun, celebrating its return. These may include angelica, ash, burnet, camomile, celandine, eyebright, juniper, lovage, marigold, rosemary, tormentil, viper's bugloss and walnut.

CANDLEMAS (IMBOLC)
Ivy, heather, chamomile, bay, angelica, anise, peppermint, thyme, and also any plant that has a magical association with purification, creativity and inspiration. Cowslip and sage are good examples.

VERNAL (SPRING) EQUINOX
Tansy, marjoram, willow, crocus, cinquefoil, daffodil, vervain, lily, iris, and also any herb that flowers in spring, or has magical associations with health, purification, and growth. These include anemone, angelica, lesser celandine, colt's foot, fennel and wood sorrel.

BELTANE
Lady thistle, fern, lilac, nettle, angelica, primrose, woodruff, elder and any other herbs with the magical associations of love or prosperity. A considerable list of these is available to choose from but here are some of the easiest to obtain. Artichoke, French bean, ladies' bedstraw, birch, burdock, cherry, columbine, cowslip, foxglove, golden rod, gooseberry, groundsel, mallow and

marshmallow, dog's mercury, mint, mugwort, parsnip, peach, periwinkle, plantain, sorrel, strawberry, tansy and thyme. Rowan is strongly protective at Beltane, and, hawthorn decorates the witch's stave or stang.

SUMMER SOLSTICE
Sage, mint, hyssop, rue, fennel, verbena, hazel, dock, oak, horsetail and any other herbs with the magical association of fertility and aphrodisiac properties. Apple, catmint, hemlock, lords and ladies, mandrake and orache or goosefoot are examples, though please remember that none of these herbs should be taken internally. They are to be employed for their magical powers only. Chicory, hemlock, English mandrake and lords and ladies, in particular, are all dangerously poisonous if consumed.

LAMMAS (LUGHNASADH)
Goldenrod, yarrow, comfrey, milkweed, corn, oak, wheat, and any other grain or seed that represents the harvest and good fortune. Heather and clover are among the best-known examples. In England broom has also been recognized as a symbol of good luck at a wedding.

AUTUMN EQUINOX (MABON)
Marigold, sage, thistle, rosehips, acorns, ferns, aster, milkweed, oak, and any other plants that are associated with death and the end of the cycle. The best known of these in Britain is the yew, but also remember periwinkle, rosemary, thyme, willow and lilac. In Greek legend aconite, dangerously poisonous, was a plant of the underworld. In the East, chrysanthemum is most commonly linked with death and funeral rites.

Sacrifice:
a rite of reverence

In bygone times, many religions were dominated by sacrifical rituals in which live animals and, not infrequently, human beings were offered to the gods. Fortunately this kind of appeasement went out of fashion centuries ago and it has largely been replaced by allegory.

We perform spiritual or mental exercises that constitute a kind of inner sacrifice which is just as potent as the exercise of slaughtering a goat or a chicken on the altar used to be. The logic of sacrifice has often been quite a simple one. In India, for example, the worshipper recognizes that work earns reward in wages, food, clothing and other necessities. It follows that a different kind of activity on behalf of a deity will earn spiritual returns. Sacrifice and reward are seen as a kind of contractual exchange and it is understood that the deities are dependent on sacrifice just as much as the person making it is dependent on the spiritual powers for their response.

Fire is seen not only to purify but also to send the sacrificial object aloft to the heavens as smoke. It requires a sacred fire altar built with bricks or some other suitable material which is demolished after use, as well as a number of other essential ingredients. The Goddess or God who is to receive the sacrifice must be named and a suitable sacrificial object or material decided upon. The

Preparing a grimoire

■ A witch's *Herbal Grimoire* lists herbs for use on practically every ritual occasion. You can obtain one of these at any occult bookshop (see page 140). The choice of herbs is very much an individual one, but let us take, for example, the ingredients for a midsummer offering. Herbals will frequently suggest the use of lavender, chamomile, St John's wort and vervain on this occasion. Collect the ingredients

Sacrifices of a symbolic nature can be used to demonstrate our reverence to the spiritual world without the need to spill blood or perform acts of brutality.

ceremony of offering the sacrifice to the deity and the prayer that accompanies it, whether private or open, must form part of a properly conducted ritual or the whole thing becomes worthless.

In our alternative ceremonies we can make offerings in a number of ways. An incense-burner is perhaps the simplest means of conveying our invocations to the deities, and we can use the flame in a crucible to burn small objects such as paper models, messages, dried flowers, herbs and so on. It is important to remember, however, that if we are conducting a sacrifice away from home, any open fire must be controlled and permission must be obtained before lighting it.

and place them in a small square of cloth. As you do so, mentally send all your problems, worries, fears and troubles into the little pile of herbs, then gather up the corners of the cloth and tie it into a pouch with some red string or ribbon. At the appropriate moment in your ceremony throw the pouch on to your fire or incense crucible, saying words similar to:

I banish you by the powers
of the Goddess and God!
I banish you by the powers
of the Sun, Moon and Stars!
I banish you by the powers
of Earth, Air, Fire and Water!

The value
of prayer

Very little in our alternative ceremony is formalized, and prayer is no exception. Don't imagine that there is a book of 'set' prayers like the Lord's Prayer of the Christian faith, because such a thing does not exist.

This means that we are free to create our own prayers, which we offer time after time, and that they can be personal offerings which place emphasis on the individual rather than being part of an 'establishment repertoire'. Nonetheless the way in which pagans employ prayer is much like that of Christianity or other formal religions.

For Wiccans prayer is the means of talking to the Goddess or God, asking for help and advice, discussing their worries and problems, offering praise or apology as is seen fit. A key phrase in Wicca is 'Blessed be' and it forms the opening of many pagan prayers and invocations. What follows in the prayer will depend largely on one's beliefs and needs of the moment.

You may wish, on a beautiful morning, to offer praise to the Goddess and God of nature for all the wondrous aspects of life around you. Use your eyes to pick out birds, animals, flowers, trees, hills, flowing or still water, and give your thanks for each of these. Ask the blessing of the deities upon them. Think of them as notes in the music of life that are, like us, indispensable parts of the great harmony of the earth.

Eastern wisdom

In the East attitudes to prayer are somewhat different from those in the West, since Buddhists, for example, do not recognize transcendent gods and goddesses who stand distinct and separate from humankind but believe in a transformation of consciousness. The aim is to achieve enlightenment that breaks the painful cycle or 'Wheel' of death and rebirth and leads us to ultimate bliss or *nirvana*. The key lies in a combination of meditation in order to bring enlightenment, and self-denial of material things. Gautama Buddha, the founder of Buddhism, believed we are prevented from understanding true reality because we are controlled by material values. Perfect enlightenment, he argued, requires us to vanquish self. When this is achieved we may be released from the 'Wheel'.

One of the aids to meditation, which in turn is one of the gateways to enlightenment, is the chanting of a *mantra*, a prayer which consists of a sequence of syllables that may or may not possess intelligible meaning. The best known *mantra* is 'OM' or 'AUM', a sound made up of three letters representing the great deities Brahma, Vishnu and Shiva.

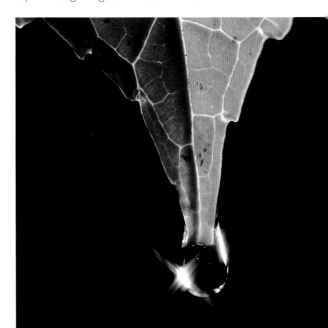

Why should I fast and how?

■ Another way to spiritual fulfilment is through fasting. Thousands of years ago fasting, as an ingredient of religious rite, was intended to reduce the activities of the body to a state comparable with death and to focus the practitioner on the spiritual world to the exclusion of the material. It was also, conversely, practised during fertility rites, as a magical device to avert disaster and as a form of penance for wrongdoing. Later, fasting became associated with spiritual purification and today it is still recognized as a means to rid ourselves of the impurities of the material world, provided that it is approached sensibly. If you decide to enter a fast, it should be one of partial abstinence rather than total. It can be carried out on certain days or by rejecting particular foods, perhaps those that are rich or self-indulgent, for a period of time. In its way vegetarianism is a form of fasting. In other words, make the discipline more a symbolic act than real physical deprivation of the food that constitutes important nutrition.

Rituals
for healing

In our modern world of medical breakthroughs we have become somewhat complacent about the treatment of illness. Increasingly, however, we are coming to the realization that medical science cannot always provide the answers.

Our problems of mind and body can sometimes be dealt with by other means, and the origins of these techniques are often buried deep in our cultural past.

The power of spirit guides

The Navajo Indians of North America believe strongly that sickness can be a result of our falling out of harmony with the natural world, within which we are not only individuals but also an integral part. Navajos place strong reliance on ceremonial chants to treat disease, since these songs, known as chantways, are believed to restore vital balance and harmony. Each chantway has been given to the Indians by the spirits and relates to a specific imbalance or disharmony. The healing ceremony begins with a blessing similar to the one on page 31 but with words tailored to the identity and needs of the sick person. Navajos call this introductory rite a blessingway. It should include a simple ritual object in the form of a small cloth bag containing material from a sacred site; the Indians know this as a mountain soil bundle. If you

The art of faith healing?

■ Faith healing is an ancient art once practised amongst the Greeks and Romans who believed that the God of medicine, Aesculapius, would bring cures to those who prayed to him.

■ By the third Christian century the faith in the curative power of holy relics had become extraordinarily strong.

The rite of spiritual
healing is a matter of faith,
both for practitioner and
patient, to return the body
to its correct harmonies
and to dispel 'dis-ease'.

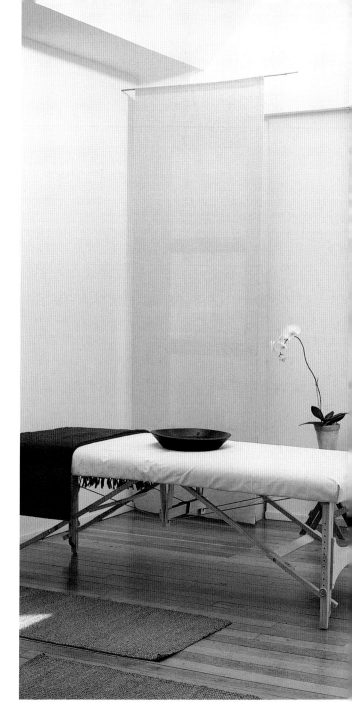

are to make your own sacred bundle, do remember that most ancient sites of worship in Europe and the UK carry strict and essential rules about removal of material. A very small amount of dirt or a single pebble will suffice. The bundle should be placed in contact with the person to be healed, as close as possible to the site of the sickness. The blessingway thus lays the foundation for the healing chant and you will need to compose this according to the nature of the sickness presented.

A modern spiritual healer will generally follow similar principles of faith, calling initially, by means of prayer, on the help of a guide or mentor from the 'other world' for whom he or she acts as a medium. Practitioners of healing generally begin by conducting a ceremony of cleansing to eliminate negative energies. They may then move into a state of altered consciousness or 'trance' in which they are directed by their spirit mentors to seek out those spiritual elements in the patient that, through trauma of one kind or another, have lost their normal harmony. They have been taken out of the ordinary into the extraordinary, in other words they have become disassociated. These elements are led back into normal harmony when the medium taps into the powers of the spirit guide and draws them into their proper association.

Spiritual healers frequently describe the sensation of power coming to their hands in the form of tingling. The hands are laid gently either upon the patient or close but without touching. The psychic centres of energy or *chakras* (see pages 128–9) are often, though not always, the areas of work, and healers report that they are directed by their spiritual mentors as to which of the *chakras* to concentrate on. A spiritual healer may also use pressure points similar to those used in acupuncture.

In the more widely publicized demonstrations of faith healing, the medium often places their hands over the top of the patient's head, or some other area of the body. The important principle to understand is that the hands are merely acting as a channel for psychic power emanating from the spirit guide, and that this is helped on its way through the intense mental concentration of the medium. In response the patient usually reports sensations of heat or cold, and there may be an improvement in the affected area of the body as the blockage of the energy pathways is removed and harmony restored.

Alleviating stress
through meditation

Since very early times, probably not less than 4,000 years ago, certain people living in India have practised the discipline of yoga. In the modern world it is regarded as one of the best ways of alleviating stress, but this was not its original purpose.

Sometime before 500 CE the details were written into a book called the *Yoga-sutra* by the great Hindu philosopher Patanjali. He described the aim of the practitioner, the *yogi*, as the ceasing of all conscious thoughts through physical training and will-power, allowing the subconscious freedom to achieve spiritual fulfilment and the discovery of the ultimate reality.

The adoption of yoga in the West

The *yoga* discipline is said to stem from the teaching of the Supreme Lord, the *mahayogi*, Shiva, and for the true student the mental and physical disciplines that we see demonstrated in the familiar postures and hand gestures are coupled with a life of austerity and rejection of earthly desires. In modern Western life, the word *yoga* has become used to describe various spiritual practices of meditation which, in reality, have little in common with the original classical Indian concept of *sankhya yoga* and are generally referred to as *hatha yoga*. Classical yoga is popular, today, among a broad mass of Hindu worshippers, but the adaptation to Western needs renders *hatha yoga* no less valuable to you and me as a means of cleansing the mind and seeing beyond the stresses of modern living.

In practice, the classical yoga on which our westernized discipline is based requires training in a number of routines, part physical and part mental. The most important of these is breath control, known as *pranayama*,

Diet and yoga

■ Diet is also important in achieving good results with yoga. Salt and strong-flavoured food should be avoided. Milk is said to be the ideal food for yogis, though of course milk alone does not provide an adequate diet. Any diet must be approached sensibly and on sound medical advice. The yogic diet is essentially vegetarian and consists of pure, simple foods that are easily digested. Fruits, vegetables, seeds, nuts and grains are readily assimilated by the body and render the mind calm.

directing the vital breaths through six or seven body centres or *chakras* (see pages 128–9), withdrawing the senses from material stimuli, suspending mental activity and reciting mantras such as 'OM' (see page 120). Physically, *yoga* requires adoption of certain body positions known as *asanas* during meditation, permitting the person to remain motionless in comparative comfort for long periods of time without falling asleep or straining. The *hatha yoga* manual lists eighty-four bodily positions with varying degrees of difficulty, but any of these will serve provided it allows the person to practise continued concentration and meditation.

The power of yoga

Most people never pass beyond the basic meditation exercises, but the most advanced *yogis* are claimed to have reached an extraordinary state of control. It allows them to reduce their body metabolism so that the heartbeat falls to a more or less imperceptible level and they appear not to be breathing at all. In this state all fear of dying is said to have been lost and the *yogi* has begun a process of purification. In this state he or she is said to be able to perform miraculous acts including expanding to an enormous size, shrinking to that of a grain of sand or even becoming wholly invisible, as well as leaving the body for temporary periods.

In order to achieve full mental realization we are instructed to follow three essential steps. First we must concentrate our minds towards a single subject or picture. This is a process called *dharana*. If we manage to achieve the total focus on one topic, we must stay that way! Next comes *dhyana*, demanding that our mental picture remains concentrated and unchanged. Finally, and this is probably the hardest exercise, we are required through *samadhi* to lose the physical form of our concentrated image until it becomes no more than an abstract understanding.

Basic yoga positions

Yoga involves a combination of physical control and meditation techniques. When these are properly applied they permit a state of release and liberation from the material world, bringing both insight and personal peace.

The baddha kona-asana

This is one of the easiest yoga positions for aiding meditation and keeping the body healthy. Sit on the floor with your legs straight out in front of you. Try to keep your back straight and your head upright. Place your palms flat on top of each thigh and then, taking hold of your toes with each hand, draw your feet up towards your bottom while bending the knees outwards.

If you are really supple you should now be able to press down on your thighs so that the outer edge of each knee and calf are in contact with the floor and your heels are against your bottom with the little toes touching one another. *Never strain to achieve this posture and do not hold the position for longer than is comfortable, certainly not for more than two minutes.*

When you release the posture, stretch the legs out as before with your palms resting on your thighs. The exercise can be repeated two or three times and should be practised as often as possible.

What do I do with my hands?

■ There are three classical positions for the hands in association with the *padma asana*. The first is to rest the hands on the heels, palms up, one over the other. The second is to place the palms facing downwards on the knees. The third is a classic position that you will see adopted in many sculptures of Hindu gods and goddesses. It is a gesture known as the *chinmudra*, which means 'reflection-hand-posture', symbolizing

The ardha padma-asana

This is called the Half Lotus Posture. The Lotus is one of the classic *yoga* positions identified with meditation but it is best for someone new to *yoga* to start with a slightly easier version. Sit on the floor, legs straight out in front of you, back straight, shoulders level and head upright. Now bend your right knee and, taking hold of the foot with both hands, draw it up so that it rests on top of your left thigh as close to your hip as possible. Next bend your left knee and draw the foot up so that it rests *under* the right thigh. Each knee and calf should now be resting on the floor, with the sole of the right foot pointing upwards. With your back straight but not rigid, hold the position for a maximum of two minutes and then relax by placing your legs straight out in front of you, palms resting on thighs. Now alternate the legs so that your left foot is drawn up on to your right thigh. Repeat the positions two or three times.

The padma-asana

You should not attempt to reach this posture unless you are first reasonably comfortable with the previous two that I have described. It is the posture often adopted by the Buddha. Sit on the floor and draw the right foot up on to the left thigh in the same position as you adopted for the Half Lotus. Now take the left foot in the right and draw it up over the right thigh. The soles of both feet should now be pointing upwards, heels in contact with your pelvic area and knees and calves parallel with the floor.

The garuda-asana

This is comparatively easy. Stand, feet together, and then bring up your left foot and tuck it behind your right leg, with your left thigh resting on your right thigh. Cross your arms left over right and join your palms with the fingers pointing upwards. Inhale and hold, then repeat the position using your right foot first.

realization of the absolute truth. Turn the palms up and place the backs of the hands on the knees, right hand to right knee, left to left. Now join the tips of the index finger and the thumb in order to form a ring. Extend the remaining fingers straight. *Chinmudra* is an extension of the *mukulamudra* or 'bud' posture symbolizing love, where the tips of the fingers and thumb come together like an unopened flower.

Chakras
and breathing

A chakra is simply an invisible energy centre of the body that can be envisaged in the form of a pulsating light, each being identified by a different colour of the spectrum. Many of these centres have been identified, but there are seven major recognized chakras.

The *muladhara chakra* is located at the base of the spine and is associated with the colour red. The *svadistthana chakra* is in the sacral region of the spine near the pelvis and is orange. The *manipura chakra* lies at the solar plexus and is yellow. The *anahata chakra* lies at the centre of the breast bone and is emerald green. The *visuddi chakra* in the throat is blue. The *ajna chakra* in the centre of the forehead takes the colour violet. Finally, the *sahasara chakra* on the crown of the head is recognized by a pure white light.

Concentrating on the opening of the *chakras* is a recognized method of altering our inner consciousness and controlling our psychic energies. The order in which the *chakras* are opened can be ascending or descending, i.e. you can start with either the *sahasara* or the *muladhara*. Many people find it easiest to begin at the base of the spine and work upwards, but the action should then progress in sequence. It is best to conduct this ritual in a group where one person acts as leader; that person ideally should possess some degree of 'sixth sense' or clairvoyance so that they can recognize when each member of the group has managed to open a particular energy centre.

In her book *Wicca*, Vivianne Crowley advises that we should envisage the circle of light that corresponds with each *chakra* growing, spinning around and becoming brighter until it covers the whole area of the body. We must then imagine that energy is being sucked into the spinning *chakra* rather like water into a vortex until it fills our bodies. The suggestion is that by starting with the lowest *chakra* at the base of the spine and working upwards we can envisage our bodies filling with energy, like fuel pouring into a petrol tank! At each stage in the filling process we should return to the *chakra* at the base of the spine and begin to suck in more energy through the successive energy centres until, eventually, energy is shooting like a stream of brilliant white light through the crown of our head.

At the end of the ritual it is important that we also close the *chakras*, and one of the simplest ways that can we do this is by feasting. This will serve to 'earth' the energies that have been raised.

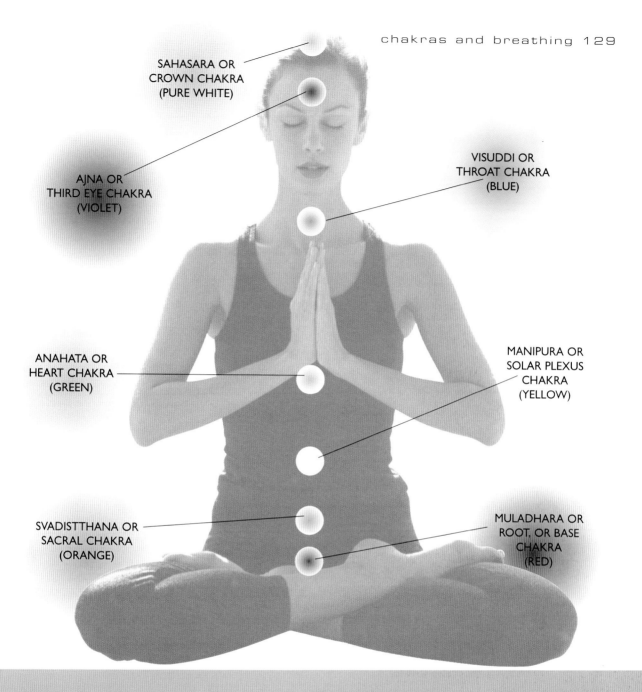

SAHASARA OR
CROWN CHAKRA
(PURE WHITE)

AJNA OR
THIRD EYE CHAKRA
(VIOLET)

VISUDDI OR
THROAT CHAKRA
(BLUE)

ANAHATA OR
HEART CHAKRA
(GREEN)

MANIPURA OR
SOLAR PLEXUS
CHAKRA
(YELLOW)

SVADISTTHANA OR
SACRAL CHAKRA
(ORANGE)

MULADHARA OR
ROOT, OR BASE
CHAKRA
(RED)

Breath control

■ The way in which we breathe, particularly during meditation, is essential for directing our psychic energies. Eastern techniques, such as those practised in Taoism (see pages 112–3), require the breathing to be soft and slow, with the mouth closed and the nose used for both inhaling and exhaling. People with respiratory problems are, however, allowed to use mouth breathing. It is important when practising breathing techniques that they feel comfortable. If any disorientation is experienced the action must be stopped.

■ It is important to guide the speed of breathing and the flow of breath within the body, though this should never be forced, and the simplest method is to count the number of inhalations and exhalations. You may wonder what is the point of this exercise? If we concentrate the conscious mind on something as repetitive as our breathing it produces a similar result to the use of a mantra like 'OM'. Our superficial mind is distracted and this permits our subsconscious mind to rise up, with the liberation of our psychic channels.

The power
of dance

We have already discussed the importance of the spiral dance in Wicca as a means of awakening the subconscious mind and enabling us to draw upon and concentrate psychic energy.

Dance, however, is also part of the age-old quintessence of ritual for another reason. Together with chant it formalizes the stages of a sacred ceremony. We can discover examples of its use as far back as Ice Age times, 20,000 years ago. In a deep cavern known as Trois Frères, in the Dordogne region of south-west France, there is preserved a bizarre engraved image that has been dubbed 'The Sorcerer'. It is half human, half animal, and it stands in a curious fashion, crouched forward in such a way that, if motionless, it would topple on its face. In fact it exudes a sense of frenetic movement and it is believed to be one of the earliest representations of a dancing priest, dressed in an animal costume to represent the Lord of the Hunt.

In another of the deep caverns, Tuc d'Audoubert, the footprints of children have been immortalized in the once soft clay floor. They fan out in six clear rows towards the mouth of an underground chamber and archaeologists have established that *only the heels* made contact with the ground. Were these children from the misty edge of prehistory dancing and trying to emulate the steps of the animal spirits they revered so deeply?

In more recent times, through the medium of Hollywood westerns, the rainmaking ceremonies of American Indians have become some of the best-known ritual dances, but many tribal customs involve similar rites. To invoke the spirits to generate rain, one of the most widely practised dances in tribal groups involves carrying a small branch that is regularly dipped into a container of water as the dancers move around the sacred circle. The

'Summer is a comin' in'

Summer is a comin' in – Loudly sing cuckoo
Groweth seed and bloweth mead and springeth wood
Sing cuckoo!
Ewe bleateth after lamb, loweth after calf the cow.
Bullock starteth, buck to fern goeth. Merry sing cuckoo!
Cuckoo. Cuckoo. Well singest thou cuckoo – not cease thou ever now.

A traditional English song to which one can dance.

branch is shaken, sprinkling the drops on the ground in a magical representation of the falling rain.

The simplest form of dance that we can copy today is the so-called circle dance, which is thought to have arisen in Ireland. It requires us to join hands and run or skip around the periphery of the sacred circle or bonfire, and perhaps also jump over the bonfire. In order to maintain a sense of rhythm, the dance can be accompanied by the dancers carrying tambourines or *sistrum* rattles, or someone can mark time with a drum. In order to join in ritual dancing we do not, you will be relieved to know, need to learn the complicated steps of a sacred foxtrot!

In Somerset, in southern England, there is a traditional meeting dance, a special form of the spiral dance used by

pagans at the beginning of a ritual (see pages 18–19). Everyone joins hands in the circle, men and women alternating. Each faces outwards and begins to dance anti-clockwise or widdershins in the direction of death, while the men keep their left heel clear of the ground. This makes them hobble, imitating the bull god, Baal, who died and was restored as the sacred king. The priestess suddenly releases her left hand and leads the dance inwards in a gradual spiral until the dancers have come together in the centre of the circle. She turns to her right and kisses the man next to her in a symbolic awakening to new life, before leading the dancers in an expanding clockwise or deosil spiral following the sun and the rebirth of life. Each woman likewise kisses a man as she passes him.

The power
of chanting

We can also chant as we dance to increase our change in mental perception and to heighten our ability to generate psychic energy.

The Somerset Meeting Dance (described on page 131) is accompanied by the words, 'Thout, tout a tout, throughout and about', but for pagans the best-known and most oft-recited chant is the Witches' Rune. This is to be found in the *Book of Shadows*, the handbook of modern Wicca which was first published in 1959 and which originates from a manuscript prepared by one of the great pioneers of pagan revival in England, Gerald Gardner. He borrowed much of the material from ancient sources, including classical mythology, Celtic fertility rites and Rosicrucianism, as well as from a more recent fellow occultist, Aleister Crowley.

You may wonder why a collection of meaningless chanted words like the closing verse of the Witches' Rune are employed at all. A rune is simply a magical rhyme based on the old runic alphabet of the Angles and Saxons. Each runic letter has a special magical meaning, and runes were often carved or engraved on spears and sword handles to give the weapons magical potency. As we have already discussed, one of the forms of chant most employed in eastern religions is the *mantra*, often involving a single syllable such as 'OM' repeated over and over. The 'OM' *mantra* is a primaeval sound through which the Supreme Being can be reached. One of the great teaching books of ancient Indian religion, the *Atharvaveda*, includes *mantras* for and against everything, from sickness to love to hatred!

Arguably the main purpose in ritual of a rune or *mantra* is to occupy the conscious mind and keep it distracted, allowing the subconscious or 'deep mind' to bubble up to the surface and do its work while severing the ordinary relationship with reality. One of the advantages for someone keen to practise alternative ritual is that the actual words of the chant are fairly immaterial and they can be invented to suit the purpose. If, for example, you are invoking a particular spirit, it is quite acceptable to use just the name of the spirit repeated over and over.

The American pagan Starhawk encourages us to experiment with rhythm and a combination of musical notes, rearranging and altering them to make them thoroughly individual and personal. The pagan anthropologist Tanya Luhrmann suggests an elaboration, a technique of wordless chanting or 'tuning' where one person hums or sings a single note. The rest of the group joins in with variations of pitch and intonation to produce an eerie sound that rises and falls without a melody and which most closely resembles the song of a whale.

The Witches' Rune

Darksome night and shining moon
East then South then West then North
Harken to the Witches' Rune,
Here we come to call thee forth.

Earth and Fire, Air and Water
Wand and pentacle and sword
Work ye unto our desire
And harken ye unto our word.

Cord and censer, scourge and knife
Powers of the witches' blade
Waken all ye unto life
And come ye as the charm is made.

Queen of Heaven, Queen of Hell
Horned hunter of the night
Lend your power unto our spell
And work our will by magic rite.

By all the powers of land and sea
By all the might of moon and sun
As we do will so mote it be
Chant the spell and be it done

Eko, eko Azarak
Eko, eko Zamilak
Eko, eko Cernunnos
Eko, eko Aradia.

Eastern
ritual techniques

Much of our alternative ceremony has, at one time or another, been copied from Far Eastern traditions. The wisdom gained first by Chinese and Japanese philosophers was learned by travellers from the West and brought back, to our advantage.

There are fundamental differences in approach, however, that we can follow or not as we wish. Ancestor spirits are the main objects of propitiation, and these entities are not regarded as mere 'ghosts' floating around in the ether but as spirits that continue a working relationship with their living descendants.

Fasting

In the East the benefits of fasting, in order to rid the body and spiritual being of impurities, have been known for centuries, though the regimes have often been far more severe than we would, or should, wish to emulate. Before Gautama Buddha recognized the value of reasonable compromise, he fasted almost to death, eating no more than a single grain of rice a day in the belief that bodily self-mortification was a long-term discipline that would lead to spiritual perfection. Do not attempt to emulate this! Doctors are agreed that rigorous fasting can be harmful. The Buddha himself was to reject the idea of total denial, the abstinence practised by the extreme ascetic, and he then taught the Middle

The importance of fasting

■ Fasts have been used to press home a political message (Mahatma Gandhi), to avert disaster (Native American tribes) and to appease the gods (Aztecs and Incas of Sub and Central America).

■ For the Hebrews of the Old Testament, fasting was a means of humbling oneself before God, but the practice probably began with rites of mourning.

Focusing your eyes on a tranquil and beautiful image, like petals floating in a bowl, can create the right conditions for emptying the mind and bringing inner calm.

Way, which recognizes that the body must remain fit and healthy in order to sustain the mental rigours necessary to progress towards enlightenment.

Healing

We tend to associate alternative healing techniques from the Far East with acupuncture, but in China a more accessible physical therapy in the form of massage is used to work on 'internal strengthening' of the body. Stroking and kneading the main chakras, energy channels of the body that we have also learnt about from Eastern practitioners, can help to open blockages in these areas, but Chinese therapists tend to work in the opposite direction to that most frequently followed in the West. Hence a specified *chakra* is opened by working on the energy gateway above it rather than below.

Stroking and massage are examples of external treatment, but the spiritual training of Chinese Taoists also includes the development of deeper therapies known as 'internal martial arts'. At least one form of this therapy, *t'ai-chi ch'uan*, which translates obscurely as 'the ultimate fist', has now become very popular in the West but it does not stand alone. There are at least three others, set at varying degrees of difficulty. Most of the disciplines involve slow, controlled movements of the body linked with deep mental concentration. The effect is to stretch the tendons, start the joints moving properly, relax the muscles and improve circulation.

Meditation

Disciples of Taoism use meditation to encourage health and long life but also to reach the highest levels of spiritual development. One of the techniques they practise is slow breathing in order to concentrate the mind, to prevent stray thoughts and to draw us away from what is happening around us in the material world. The basic idea is to stop thoughts, emotions and sensations before they happen so that the mind becomes totally still. One way of achieving this 'mind emptying' that we can follow is by regulating our breathing (see pages 124–5). Practitioners who have reached the highest level of spiritual development, in Taoism and Buddhism, are able to reduce breathing in and out from about sixteen or twenty cycles per minute down to three or four. It is worth developing this technique as a meditation tool *but it must be acquired gradually.*

Posture is important too. Most Taoists prefer to sit on the floor with the legs crossed while meditating, though they agree that it is also possible to meditate satisfactorily while sitting in a chair, walking or standing.

Conclusion

During the last fifty years or so we have come a very long way in achieving the freedom, as individuals, to worship spiritual powers according to our own wishes.

It no longer matters whether we offer reverence and prayers to a Christian God, a pagan goddess, or to no particular numinary at all. We are no longer restricted in our beliefs, and we are permitted to conduct our religious ceremonies in the manner that meets our personal needs and aspirations without fear of redress.

We owe a tremendous debt of gratitude to men and women like Gerald Gardner and Doreen Valiente who strove to overcome social stigma and criminal charge not so many years ago. It was only in 1951 that the Fraudulent Mediums Act in the United Kingdom finally saw an end to the prospect of state prosecution against anyone accused of possessing magical powers. This all-encompassing term could be levelled at any witch or pagan practitioner. In North America restrictive laws were repealed at about the same time. The high priestess Maxine Sanders once described to me how, as a teenager who had chosen to become a witch in Cheshire, she had stones thrown at her in the street and attempts were made to set her parents' house on fire. Her immediate family disowned her.

Many of the people who decide to follow a non-orthodox religion and, for example, choose to get married by an alternative ceremony, still face disapproval, particularly from members of the older generation. The movement towards general acceptance of spiritual freedom to reach understanding of the meaning of our lives as we see fit is, however, growing in strength year by year in spite of the often vigorous resistance of the Christian establishment.

For those of us who possess the courage and the inspiration to go beyond the confines of convention and seek our gods in our own way, the experience can bring great rewards. Several years ago I spent time on the Isle of Arran in the Firth of Clyde. Arran offers its tourist beaches but, by turning inland, it is possible to discover places of great solitude which, in the remote past, have overseen arcane ceremony and worship. Once I came upon a stone circle of immense age. To stand in the presence of extraordinary monuments to a forgotten faith was, for me, an experience both humbling and uplifting.

One of my favourite walks on a summer evening as twilight approaches is to wander up the lane and across the fields to a small piece of ancient woodland where, in springtime, a carpet of bluebells and primroses erupts. The pathway takes one past the place where my neighbour's partner was buried recently. The serene grave, overlooking the valley of the river Axe, is truly a small piece of paradise. She is, of course, much loved and greatly missed by those closest to her but her burial place stands as an intimate reminder to all of us that she was, and is still, an integral part of our community. No memorial in a churchyard or a conventional cemetery could ever compete with the natural perfection of her final place of rest. If I had my time over again I guess that I would elect to make my deepest personal commitments in such a spot.

One small rite of passage is destined to become a tradition in our village, a way of celebrating the dawn of each new year. It costs us little and does not bind us to any particular faith or creed, only to each other with the priceless bond of friendship. As midnight approached at the turn of the millennium we all climbed the beacon hill. There, with a vast panoramic view of stars and twinkling lamps before us, we lit a bonfire and drank coffee and waited. As midnight came we shook hands and kissed and welcomed in another year. We shall, I know, be repeating our alternative ceremony for years to come and for as long as our legs will carry us up to those starry heights.

The Law

In England and Scotland the last Witchcraft Act of 1736, under which one could technically have been prosecuted for conducting alternative religious ceremonies, was repealed in 1951, and this led to a similar change in legislation in North America.

Today religious freedom is generally accepted in most countries of the world including those of the old communist bloc. This freedom is enshrined in Article 18 of the Universal Declaration of Human Rights (see page 8). The main caveats to bear in mind are whether or not our alternative ceremonies cause damage or harm to other people or their property, and we should also be guarded against committing acts that are likely to cause public offence or a breach of the peace. In addition we should be aware of legislation such as the Wildlife and Countryside Act of 1981, which in England protects a wide list of animals and plants that might be affected by our activities. In the United States there are still a number of laws in force governing spiritualism and fortune-telling but these vary from state to state.

What you elect to do in the privacy of your home or garden carries less responsibility than a ceremony you conduct in a public place or on someone else's private property. Remember that very few parts of the United Kingdom can be classed as common land, and those that can often have old restrictive laws attached to them. If you carry out any kind of ceremony on land under ownership, including such large tracts as those held by the Forestry Commission, the National Parks and the National Trust, you will almost certainly need a permit, possibly requiring you to take out public liability insurance cover. Activities such as lighting fires for a sacrifice will, almost inevitably, not be permitted.

Among organizations to which you may choose to refer for further advice about your rights under the law, the Pagan Federation (see page 140) is an important 'first call'. The Federation will not only advise you on your legal position but will put you in touch with other organizations worldwide. The Federation abides by three fundamental rules of conduct, ratified by its Council in 1995:

1. Love for and kinship with nature, reverence for the life force and its ever-renewing cycles of life and death.

2. A positive morality, in which the individual is responsible for the discovery and development of their true nature in harmony with the outer world and community. This is often expressed as 'Do what you will, as long as it harms none'.

3. Recognition of the Divine, which transcends gender, acknowledging both the female and male aspect of Deity.

Liferites

Throughout this book I have mentioned an organization called Liferites (see page 140). It may be that you feel insufficient confidence to conduct an alternative ceremony yourself, in which case professional help may be at hand depending upon where you live. Certain rites of passage are, inevitably, going to be more highly emotive and sensitive matters than others, and the most strident example is a funeral ceremony. Death is not the most straightforward context for performing an alternative ceremony. It carries enormous emotional weight and the wishes of many people have to be considered, so arranging an alternative funeral on your own can present problems.

Liferites is based in the United Kingdom and was established in 1998 by Cheryl and Iain Menzies-Runciman, and Lum'Rhin Dharvu. It is non-profit-making and is funded by annual subscription and donations; monies received are used to defray administrative, training and other expenses. Its committed purpose is to serve the needs of people whose choice it is to follow a non-denominational spirituality. This generally means a pagan, nature-based belief, but Liferites also caters for those of us who have no specific beliefs, and their declared aim is to respect the spiritual path of the individual without judgement. It is very much a hands-on organization offering practical advice and guidance under four basic principles – Professionalism, Service, Respect and Responsibility. The aim is always to work with integrity and openness within these principles.

Currently Liferites has about twenty registered celebrants from most nature-based and pagan spiritual paths, together with those who will conduct eclectic spiritual and non-religious ceremonies. These experienced people are based mainly in the south of England but are often willing to travel further afield in order to cover those areas not already served. Most are interactive workers and will attend those in hospital or the terminally ill to provide comfort, practical help, respite nights for carers and many other areas of assistance, though not medical support.

Liferites is unique. There is, regrettably, no comparable organization in the United States or continental Europe, and so popular have its activities become that one of its founder members has recently begun officiating at ceremonies in the United States. The organization offers a whole range of services, including information leaflets covering rites of passage and life celebrations such as births, namings, puberty, joinings, menopause, eldership and passings. They will, for example, guide you through the requirements of law surrounding marriage or death, and part of the training for those who wish to work with the organization is to spend time with local funeral directors and crematoria staff, to improve the understanding of the legalities of the death process. If they find that they cannot help you themselves in a given situation they will endeavour to introduce you to an organization that is better suited to your needs.

Useful information

USEFUL ADDRESSES

ASLAN AND THE
FRIENDS OF THE
ROLLRIGHT STONES
PO Box 333
Banbury
Oxon
OX16 8XA
UK

THE PAGAN
FEDERATION
BM Box 7097
London
WC1N 3XX
UK

THE BRITISH DRUID
ORDER
PO Box 29
St Leonards on Sea
East Sussex
TN37 7YP
UK

LIFERITES
PO Box 101
Aldershot
Surrey
GU11 3UN
UK
e-mail: info@Liferites.org.

SKY LODGE
PO Box 121
Ovando
Massachussetts
MT 59854
USA
www.geocities.com/Hear
tland/plains/Worldwidew
heatweavers

HAND PAINTING

Kits for hand painting
can be bought at occult
bookshops such as:
Atlantis Bookshop
49a Museum Street
London WC1
UK
Tel 020 7405 2120

BURIALS

In the UK you should
first obtain leaflet No.
D49, 'What to do after
death', from your local
DSS office or from
HMSO.

FURTHER READING

Adler, Margot, *Drawing Down the Moon*,
Beacon Press (1979)
Andersen, J C, *Myths and Legends of the Polynesians*,
Dover (1995)
Beth, Rae, *Hedgewitch – A Guide to Solitary Witchcraft*,
Robert Hale (1990)
Crowley, Vivianne, *Wicca – The old religion in the New Age*, Aquarian Press (1989)
Crowley, Vivianne, *Phoenix from the Flame*,
Aquarian Press (1994)
Luhrmann, T M, *Persuasions of the Witch's Craft*,
Picador (1989)
Joan, Liz, *Handbook for Pagan Healers*, Capall Bann (1988)
Jordan, Michael, *Gods of the Earth*, Bantam (1992)
Jordan, Michael, *Witches*, Kyle Cathie (1996)
Jordan, Michael, *Eastern Wisdom*, Carlton (1997)
Jordan, Michael, *Plants of Mystery and Magic*,
Blandford (1997)
McArthur, Margie, *WiccaCraft for Families*,
Phoenix (1994)
Slade, Paddy, *Seasonal Magic – Diary of a Village Witch*,
Capall Bann, (1997)
Slater, Herman (ed), *A Book of Pagan Rituals*,
Robert Hale (1988)
Spence, Lewis, *The Myths of North American Indians*,
Dover (1989)
Starhawk, *Dreaming the Dark*, Beacon Press (1982)
Valiente, Doreen, The Rebirth of Witchcraft, Robert
Hale (1989)
Valiente, Doreen, *An ABC of Witchcraft past and present*,
Robert Hale (1973)

Acknowledgements

Photographs copyright © as follows: Front Jacket top row from left to right: Powerstock Zefa; Collins & Brown Publishers Ltd (C&B); C&B; Conor O'Dwyer. Centre: C&B. Bottom row from left to right: C&B; David Hiser/Gettyone Stone; C&B; Fritz von der Schulenburg/The Interior Archive. Spine: Steve Taylor/Gettyone. Back jacket from left to right: C&B; Jeremy Walker/Gettyone; C&B.

p.1 Trip/S Grant; p.2 C&B; p.3 Images Colour Library; p.5 David Hiser/Gettyone; p.7 Deborah Davis/Gettyone; p.8 (l) Images Colour Library; pp.8/9 Paul Quayle/Axiom; p.9 Edward Parker; p.10 Jamus Woods; p.13 Meissner/Telegraph Colour Library (TCL); p.14 William Henry/Photonica; p.15 Carol Ford/Gettyone; p.16 William Henry/Photonica; p16-17 Darrell Gulin/Gettyone; p.18 Maximilian Stock/The Anthony Blake Photo Library; p.19 C&B; p.20 Christopher Thomas/Gettyone; p.21 Kevin Carlyon/Fortean Picture Library; p.22 and p.23 C&B; p.24 Edward Parker; p.25 Janet and Colin Bord/Fortean; p.26 Michael Jordan; p.27 A. Gin/Powerstock Photo Library; p.29 Art Wolfe/Gettyone; p.31 Georgette Douwma/TCL; p.32 The Photographers Library; p.33 Donna Day/Gettyone; p.35 Powerstock Zefa; p.36 Dale Higgins/Gettyone; p.37 Davies & Starr/Gettyone; p.38 Sophie Brandstrom/TCL; p.39 Megumi Miyatake/TCL; p.40 (t) and 41 C&B; p.40 (b) James Darell/Gettyone; pages 42 to 46 C&B; p.47 Pete Seaward/Gettyone; p.48 C&B; p.49 Matt Anker/TCL; p.50 C&B; p.51 A Kearney/TCL; p.52 C&B; p.53 Charles Krebs/Gettyone; p.55 Darrell Gulin/Gettyone; p.56 and pp.56–7 Ancient Art & Architecture; p.57 Klaus Aarsleff/Fortean; p.58 Erich Lessing/AKG; p.59 Hugh Sitton/Gettyone; p.60/61 A Kearney/TCL; p.63 Pete Seaward/Gettyone; p.64 Ray Main/Mainstream; p.65 Michelle Garrett; p.66 Edwin Remsberg/Gettyone; p.67 Edward Parker; p.68 Laurie Campbell/Gettyone; p.69 Pal Hermansen/Gettyone; p.70 and p.71 Michael Jordan; p.73 Peter Adams/TCL; pp.74/75 TCL; p.75 (top) I&V Krafft/Hoa Qui/TCL; p.76 and p.77 Powerstock Zefa; p.79 from top right clockwise: David Loftus/Gettyone; TCL; David Noton/TCL; Darrell Gulin/Gettyone; Darrell Gulin/Gettyone; Charles Krebs/Gettyone; Michael Jordan; C&B; p.80 Michael Jordan; p.81 Vera R Storman/Gettyone; p.83 Steve Dunning/TCL; p.84 David Noton/TCL; p.87 (t) Rex Butcher/Gettyone, (b) Darrell Gulin/Gettyone; p.88 Ron Thomas/TCL; p.89 John Marshall/Gettyone; p.90 Gary Holscher/Gettyone; p.91 Edward Parker; p.93–99 C&B; p.100 Images Colour Library; p.101 B Leslie/TCL: p.103 and p.104 Andrea Booher/Gettyone; p.105 (t) Darrell Gulin/Gettyone, (b) Conor O'Dwyer; p.106 TCL; p.107 Steve Bloom/TCL; p.109 Victoria Pearson/Gettyone; p.110 David Loftus/Gettyone; p.110/111 and p.111 Michael Jordan; p.112 and p.113 C&B; p.115 and p.117 Michael Jordan; p.118 and p.119 C&B; p.120 Geof du Feu/TCL; p.121 and p.122 and p.123 C&B; p.124 A & L Sinibaldi/Gettyone; p.125 Michelangelo Gratton/Gettyone; p.126 Andrea Booher/Gettyone; p.127 Andy Roberts/Gettyone; p.128 and p.129 C&B; p.131 Mark Williams/Gettyone; p.132 and 133 Images Colour Library; p.134 and p.135 C&B; p.136 David Hiser/Gettyone; p.136/7 TCL; p.137 Anne Laird/Powerstock Zefa; p.139 Jamus Woods

Flowers from The Flower Stall, Bluebird Café, London
Models on pages 2, 42–5 and 93–99 Jordana Meredith and Nick Reynolds

Index

A

Aaron 42
Aboriginals 46, 47
Adler, Margot 51
Aesculapius 122
agate 44
ageing, rites of passage 52–3
air, element 18
Alaska 61
Aleut tribe 60
altars 17, 18
amethyst 43
ancestor spirits 134
Anglo-Saxons 57, 78, 132
animism 6
Aphrodite 99
apple trees 41
Ar nDraiocht Fein 88
Arnold, Matthew 110
Artemis 75
Aryson, Amergin 88
Asatru 6
ash trees 24, 41, 90
ashes, scattering 65, 69, 71
Asia, funeral traditions 62, 64–5
ASLaN (Ancient Sacred Landscape Network) 26, 140
astrologers 102
Asynuir 104
Atharvaveda 132
Austria 99
Autumn Equinox 78, 86–7, 117
Aztecs 134

B

Baal 131
babies see birth
baby-carriers 46–7
Babylonians 75
Balder 90, 110
Belfire 80
Beltane 78, 80, 116–17
beryl 45
Beth, Rae 36, 38
birch trees 24
birth: birthstones 42–5
   celebrating birth 34–7
   ceremonies in tribal societies 46–7
   ceremony to mark conception 32–3

miscarriage and stillbirth 48–9
naming ceremonies 38–9
   planting trees for 40–1
birthstones 42–5
bonfires 80, 82
bonsai trees 41
Book of the Dead 58–9
Book of Shadows 76, 132
Bragi 104
Brahma 120
breath control 129, 135
brides see marriage
Bronze Age 75, 82
Buddha, Gautama 120, 134–5
Buddhism 7, 62, 65, 112–13, 120, 134–5
burial ceremonies see death
burial sites 56–7
Burma 62

C

Canada 50–1
Candlemas 78
candles 18, 36
Carnac 26
carnelian 44
Celts 10
   burial 57
   fertility rites 132
   gods 75
   midsummer 82
   sacred sites 70
   Wheel of the Year 78–9
Central America 134
Ceres 84
Cernunnos 38, 75
chai 112–13
chakras 23, 123, 124, 128–9, 135
chanting 18, 120, 122–3, 132–3
Charge of the Goddess 76–7
cherry trees 41
children 20
   puberty 50–1
   see also birth
China: birthstones 42
   funeral rites 57, 64–5
   healing 135
   purification rituals 112
   trees 40
Chinook tribe 60

Choctaw tribe 60
Christianity 6, 7, 8, 9, 10, 104, 136
   birthstones 42
   churches 71
   marriage 94
   prayer 110–11
Christmas 91
chrysolite 45
churches 71
circles: Circle of Being 17–18
   circle dance 131
   sacred circles 16–17, 30
   stone circles 26–7, 70
cleansing rituals see purification
clothes 23
coffins 62, 69
Coleridge, Samuel Taylor 86
conception 32–3
cones of energy 18–19
confetti 27
conifers 41
corn dollies 111
Corn Maiden 84
Corn Mother 84–5, 111
Corn Spirit 84
creation myths 46
Crowley, Aleister 76, 132
Crowley, Vivianne 38, 50–1, 76, 100, 128
Culpeper, Nicholas 116
Cunningham, Scott 83
Czechoslovakia 57

D

Dalhousie, Earls of 41
dance 130–1
   burial ceremonies 61
   maypoles 80, 111
   spiral dance 19, 131
Dayak tribes 46–7
death 54–71
   Chinese and Japanese funeral rites 64–5
   Eastern traditions 62
   Egyptian rituals 58–9, 65
   miscarriage and stillbirth 48–9
   Native American rites 60–1
   non-denominational funerals 67
   Polynesian funeral traditions 62–3

tailoring funerals to the individual 66–7
   woodland burials 68–9
Demeter 84
Desert Moon Circle 82
Dharvu, Lum'Rhin 139
Diana 75
diet, and yoga 124
disease, healing 122–3
dolmens 26–7
Dolní Věstonice 57
Dordogne 70, 130
'drawing down the moon' 76–7
Dreamtime 46
Druids 6, 9, 11
   sacred sites 26
   Summer Solstice 82
   Winter Solstice 88

E

earth, element 18
East Anglia 57
Eastern funeral traditions 62
Eastern ritual techniques 134–5
Ecclesiastes, Book of 66
Edgewell Tree 40–1
Egypt, ancient 58–9, 65, 71, 75
elements 18
emerald 44
energy, psychic 18, 19, 128–9
England: birthday trees 40
   burial sites 57
   laws 138
Eostre 78, 86
Ephesus 75
equinoxes 76, 78, 86–7, 116, 117
Ethereans 19

F

faith healing 122, 123
Fall Equinox see Autumn Equinox
fasting 113, 121, 134–5
Fellowship of Isis 26
fertility symbols 99
Festival of the Trees 87
festivals, Wheel of the Year 78–9
fir trees 24
fire: bonfires 80

element 18
festivals 78
Indian folk marriage 103
purification rituals 112, 113
sacrifices 118–19
Yule log 90–1
flowers 27
Forest Enterprise 69
Forestry Commission 138
France 40, 70, 130
Freya 75, 105
funerals see death

G
Gandhi, Mahatma 134
Gardner, Gerald 9, 76, 132, 136
garnet 43
Germanic peoples 24, 104
Germany 40, 114–15
ghosts 61
gifts, weddings 98–9
Gill, William Wyatt 62
Goddess (Great Mother)
    Autumn Equinox 87
    Celts worship 75
    death rituals 66
    festivals 78
    invocation to 76–7
    Lammas 84, 85
    prayer 120
    Sacred Marriage 100–1
    sacred trees 111
    sacrifices 118–19
    Summer Solstice 82
    symbols 99
    Vernal Equinox 87
    Winter Solstice 88–9
    Yule log 90
gorse 82
Great Mother see Goddess
Great Lakes tribes 60
Great Rite 100–1
Greece, ancient 84, 122
Greywing, Autumn Crystal 116
grimoires 118–19
guardian spirits 47, 111, 112, 122

H
Hallowe'en 78
handfasting 27, 94

handparting 106
hands: healing 123
    painting 104–5
    yoga 126–7
harvest 84–5, 86
hawthorn 80
hazel trees 41
healing 22–3, 122–3, 135
hearths 20, 90
Hecate 66
hedgewitches 20
henna, painting hands 105
herbs 114–17, 118–19
hilltops 71, 80
Hinduism 7, 104, 113, 124
Holly King 79, 82
holly trees 41
Horned God 38, 82
Hunt-Anschutz, Stormerne 104–5
Huron tribe 60

I
Ice Age 57, 70, 75, 130
Imbolc 78, 116
Incas 134
incense 18, 119
India: folk marriage 102–3, 104
    mantras 132
    painting hands 105
    sacrifices 118
Indonesia 46–7
Inuit tribe 60, 61
Iraq 57
Ireland 70, 131
Iroquois tribe 60
Ishtar 75
Isis 75
Islam 7, 9
Israel 42
Italy 40

J
jade 42
Japan 64
jasper 43
jewellery 42
Jews 7, 9, 42
John Barleycorn 85
Josephus 42
Judaism 7, 9, 104

K
Karen people 62
Knight, Gareth 22

L
Lammas 78, 84, 85, 117
laws 138
life, creation myths 46
Liferites 14, 36, 48, 53, 68, 139, 140
Litha 82
Lithuanian prayer for trees 41
Lord of Darkness 90, 100
Lord of the Hunt 130
Lughnasadh 78, 84, 85, 117
Luhrmann, Tanya 22, 132

M
Mabon 78, 117
manhood, rites of passage 50–1
mantras 18, 111, 120, 125, 129, 132
Maoris 41, 47
marriage
    alternative celebrations 94–7
    European wedding ceremony 104–5
    Indian folk marriage 102–3, 104
    Sacred Marriage 100–1
    separation ritual 94, 106–7
    simple wedding ceremony 98–9
massage 135
May Day 80–1
maypoles 80, 111
meditation 124–5, 135
menopause 30, 52–3
menstruation 50–1
Menzies-Runciman, Cheryl and Iain 139
Mesopotamia 90
midsummer 82–3, 91, 114–15
midwinter solstice 78, 79, 88–91
Milton Keynes 11
miscarriage 48–9
moon huts 51
Moorhouse, Anthony 95
Mother Earth 75
mountains 71
mugwort 114–15

mummies 58
myths, creation 46

N
naming ceremonies 38–9
Nanticoke tribe 60
National Parks 69, 138
National Trust 26, 69, 138
Native Americans: dance 130
    fasting 134
    rites for the dead 60–1
    sacred sites 71
nature, cycle of 72–91
Navajo tribe 122–3
Nerthur 75
Netherlands 91
New Zealand 41, 47
nomads 71
Norsemen 24, 25, 90, 104, 112

O
Oak King 79, 82
oak trees 24, 41
offerings 118–19
Old Ones 36
Old Testament 42, 71
'OM' mantra 132
onyx 44
Osiris 58, 65
otherworld 56
Othin 90, 104, 105, 110

P
Padstow 80–1
Pagan Federation 21, 26, 138
painting hands 104–5
Papua New Guinea 41
Patanjali 124
Pearson, Nigel 95–7
Persia 114–15
pine trees 41
plants 114–17, 118–19
poems: for the loss of a baby 49
    from the Book of the Dead 59
Polynesians, funeral traditions 62–3
prayers 30, 110–11, 120–1
    healing 123
    Lithuanian prayer for trees 41

naming prayer 39
  for a new baby 37
  for the rites of passage 31
pregnancy, ceremony to mark
conception 32–3
priests and priestesses 10
propitiation 110–11, 134
psychic energy 18, 19, 128–9
puberty 30, 50–1
purification: fasting 121
  rituals 112–13
  sacred spaces 16–17
Pyramids 58, 71

R
Ragnarok 112
rainmaking ceremonies 130–1
reincarnation 62
relationships 92–107
Rice Mother 84
rings, wedding 104, 105
rites of passage 28–30
  conception and birth 32–49
  death and rebirth 54–71
  menopause 52–3
  puberty 50–1
Rocky Mountains 104
Rollright Stones 26
Rollright Trust 26
Roman Catholic Church 8,
  111
Romans 75, 114–15, 122
rosaries 111
rosemary 114–15, 116
Rosicrucianism 132
ruby 45
Rughs, William 85
runes 104, 132
Russia 40, 84, 91

S
Sabbats 78, 116–17
sacred sites 70–1
sacred spaces 16–17, 26–7
sacrifice 118–19
saining 38–9
salt 18, 113
Samhain 78, 116
sanctuaries 71
Sanders, Alex 9
Sanders, Maxine 136
sapphire 43
Saxons 57, 132

Scandinavia 104
Scotland 40–1, 70
separation ritual 106–7
Shamanism 6
Shiva 120, 124
Slade, Paddy 80, 86–7
solstices 78, 79, 82, 88–91,
  117
Somerset Meeting Dance 131,
  132
'The Sorcerer' 130
South Downs 71
spaces, sacred 16–17, 26–7
spiral dance 19, 131
spirit guardians 47, 111, 112,
  122
spiritual healing 123
spring 80–1
Spring Equinox 76, 78, 86–7,
  116
springs 25
standing stones 70
Starhawk 48–9, 132
stillbirth 48–9
stone circles 26–7, 70
Stonehenge 26, 71, 82
stress 124–5
'Summer is a comin' in' 130
Summer Solstice 78, 79, 82–3,
  117
Sun, Winter Solstice 88
Sutton Hoo 57
Sweden 91
symbols: fertility 99
  marriage 105

T
t'ai-chi ch'uan 135
Taoism 65, 112–13, 129, 135
Tara 70
Thor 104, 105
tools 18–19
topaz 45
Toronto 50–1
Tower of Babel 71
trees 24–5
  birth of babies 36, 38, 40–1
  burial ceremonies 66
  Festival of the Trees 87
  miscarriage and stillbirth 48
  touching wood 111
  woodland burials 68–9
  Yule log 90–1

tribal societies: birth
  ceremonies 46–7
  dance 130–1
  fasting 134
  moon huts 51
  rites for the dead 60–1
  sacred sites 71
Trois Frères cavern 130
Tuc d'Audoubert cavern 130
'tuning' 132

U
umbilical cord 41, 47
United States of America
  Autumn Equinox 78
  harvest 84
  laws 138
  Summer Solstice 82
  Winter Solstice 88
  see also Native Americans

V
Valiente, Doreen 6, 9, 76, 100,
  136
Var 104
Vernal Equinox see Spring
Equinox
vervain 114–15
Vikings 57, 75, 104
violets 86
Vishnu 120

W
water
  element 18
  holiness 18, 24–5
  at midsummer 91
  purification rituals 17, 112
weddings see marriage
wells 25
Wheel of the Year 78–9
Wicca 6, 9
  great Goddess 76–7
  handparting 106–7
  prayer 120
  Sabbats 11, 116–17
  Sacred Marriage 100–1
  Witches' Rune 132
Winter Solstice 78, 79, 88–91
Wise, Caroline 98–9
witches 8, 21, 136
Witches' Rune 132
wood see trees

woodland burials 68–9
World Ash 24, 25, 90, 111

Y
yarrow 114–15
yew trees 24, 66
Yggdrasil 24, 25, 90, 111
yoga 124–7
Yoga-sutra 124
Yule log 90–1
Yuletide 78, 116

Z
Zen Buddhism 112–13
ziggurats 71
zodiac, birthstones 42